A full listing of titles in this series appears at the close of this book

Jake: Just Learn to Worship

About the Author

Terry Young spent much of his childhood in the Middle East where his parents were missionaries. They returned to the Midlands in time for his secondary education. After university he settled in Essex, married Danielle, and together they are bringing up a family of three boys. He has been on the leadership team of his church for just over a decade, but is on the move once more.

As someone who has worked in industry for just over 16 years and travelled widely with his work, Terry identifies with many of the things that make Jacob such an interesting character.

Partnership

PARTNERSHIP GUIDES

Jake: Just Learn to Worship

Terry Young

Published for

by

PATERNOSTER PRESS

First published 2003 by Partnership and Paternoster Press

09 08 07 06 05 04 03   7 6 5 4 3 2 1

British Library Cataloguing in Publication Data
A catalogue record for this book is available from the British Library.

ISBN 0-900128-27-5

Cover design by Paulo Baigent.
Typeset by Profile, Culmdale, Rewe, Exeter.
Produced by Jeremy Mudditt Publishing Services, Carlisle,
and published by Partnership and Paternoster Press,
PO Box 300, Carlisle, Cumbria CA3 0QS.
Printed and bound in Great Britain
by Bell and Bain Ltd, Glasgow.

To my friends at Tile Kiln Chapel

Contents

Preface

Where did that come from?

A friend of mine runs a group of companies. In his time he has bought and sold companies, taken on staff and, on occasions, has had to fire a few. His wife was at a women's conference a while ago when she discovered that she and another lady there had something in common. It turned out that my friend had fired this other lady's husband. You might think that this would rather wreck the cordiality of a Christian retreat for these two women, but it didn't. The dismissal had proved a turning point for this unfortunate chap and he and his wife had both become Christians. Rather than touching a raw nerve, the encounter closed an important loop for my friend and his wife. I should think that Philemon would mean a whole lot more to them, after that. I imagine one might be able to appreciate the delicate way in which Paul writes as he sends the runaway slave Onesimus, now converted, back to his Christian master.

And there are times in life when you find yourself going through an experience that mirrors rather closely someone else's experience in scripture. Suddenly the text is alive and you are aware of nuances that you missed before. And it happened to me.

I have been experimenting in our church with group services. Together with a team of men, I was studying to deliver five Sunday morning services on Jacob. The others were James Bell, Bryan Bland, Dave Griffiths, Russell Hilton, Barry Rix and Phil Stannard. One rule of these exercises is that you cannot run one and speak – I cannot handle more than one role effectively (nor am I sure that anyone else can). So I was part of the team without being part of the delivery. I have done this type of thing before and it is hard, as the ideas come out, not to think, hey, I could have fun with this material myself. And that is partly why I have written this. But it is not the only reason.

At the same time, things were happening at work. Several months earlier, I remember my company ran a global employee

survey. One of the questions asked whether we thought we
would still be working for the company in a year's time (I
think). I thought of entering 'no' just to keep the management
on its toes. After all, who knows what will happen? However, I
had filled in questionnaires like this one before and wanted to
be as open as possible. I had no plans to leave and guessed that
I would be around for the foreseeable future. I went for 'yes'.

As the weeks passed, work became less secure. I had always
expected I was to move from the position I held, since it had
been lots of fun but a bit anomalous in the overall scheme of
things. A period of waiting and uncertainty followed and, as it
became clear what sort of role was opening up, I had serious
concerns. And around this time, there we were studying Jacob
with his uncertainties, his continual striving to find a bargaining
position.

It came to a head when Dani (my wife) said it was OK to think
about leaving. She was scared, too, but we had learnt from past
experience that being miserable at work was no fun at home
either. I had just enjoyed a couple of the most stimulating years
of my career with a boss whom I really respected. Feeling very
uncomfortable about the options ahead, I took a package to
leave instead. And on Monday evenings we were reading about
Jacob, who gets there in the end. The message coming through
seemed to be that it is hard to get it completely wrong if you
learn to worship and keep God in your sights.

Interesting things began to happen. Initially, I planned to set
up my own business. The contacts were promising and the sums
seemed to add up. When I was still contemplating leaving, I
phoned around to see who might be interested in using my
services. Someone e-mailed back asking if I would like to work
for him. We met and talked, and over the summer the sugges-
tion metamorphosised into a written offer.

In my final month of work, a professor with whom I worked
on a committee rang. He said I had expressed some interest in
moving into academia the last time we had met – was I still
interested? I explained that I was, rather. And so there was a second lead.

I had hoped that both prospects would mature at the same
time, but God's timing is not ours, as Jacob, too, discovers. I had
to be willing to let go of the industrial job to go after the academic post.

I left work after the team had delivered the series. Over the summer, one other thing happened. Someone showed some interest in another manuscript I had written. I still do not know whether or when it will be published, but it persuaded me I might make it as a writer one day. Why not get your thoughts down about Jacob in a book? Why not write it while you have the time? Why not write while you still do not know the outcome? There is a fairly hard deadline, since I have to go back to work soon. Could I write 40,000 words by then?

I have tried to write in the present. Most, but not all, the chapters were written in sequence, so sometimes my experience may take a step backward as you progress through the book. I still do not know how it will all end, although I will let you know in the last chapter.

Is this a good way to study? It is certainly a fun approach to the Bible. I hope it works for you, too, coming as it does second-hand. I guess that what you lose in the immediacy of the experience, you gain in not having to worry about how it all ends up.

And through all this, I think I have come to understand Jacob much better. His failures are my failures. His struggles are my struggles. Perhaps one day I may share in the success he makes of his relationship with God.

In the meantime, enjoy...

Acknowledgements

There are so many people who have contributed to this book in one way or another. For instance, those who worship at Tile Kiln Chapel have a tolerant approach to experiments, which makes it possible to try new things and develop new ministries. I would like to thank James, Bryan, Dave, Russell, Barry and Phil for those Mondays we spent together and for the Sundays they spent up the front. Also, Jeremy Mudditt has been such a help with his careful management of the process of bringing a manuscript to print.

There are two other people I must single out for special thanks. Without a champion, it is extremely difficult to publish these days, and Harold Rowdon has been that champion for me. Thank you, Harold. And finally, my wife, Dani has put up with so much during the creation and development of this book: I have typed when we could have talked, I have corrected proofs until two in the morning. Dani has created the space in which I have been able to work. Dani was calm when I was worried. For all this and so much more, thank you, thank you, Dani.

Introduction

So who was Jacob? He was overshadowed by his grandfather, Abraham the Friend of God, and eclipsed by his son Joseph who became Prime Minister of Egypt. And yet Jacob's story stretches over half the book of Genesis, starting with his birth in chapter 25 and concluding with his burial in chapter 50. Someone who gets that many column inches must be worth a second glance.

There are other reasons for looking at Jacob as I hope we shall see in the following chapters. Perhaps the fact that we have so much narrative enables us to understand him more as a real person. We have sketches of him as a youngish chap, as a family man, as a grandfather and as a very old man. We also see him in different situations that help us to build up a solid picture of the man as he lives his life.

And Jacob is a very real person. He wants the best out of life and, given his difficult start as the younger twin in a firstborn-takes-all society, we are immediately struck by his grit in turning around a tricky start. I love his sheer guts. Time and again he finds himself starting all over again, his opponent holding the aces, while Jacob plays a waiting game. Whether biding his time with Esau or labouring for Uncle Laban, Jacob plays a long game, a game lasting decades, in hope of a final payoff.

At home, with a dozen sons and their four mothers, we see a Jacob a little detached. My experience only stretches to a quarter of his wives and sons, so I can only guess what home life must have been like. Jacob, preoccupied perhaps with providing for an ever-widening circle of mouths to feed and with his eye still on the longer term prospect of prosperity, lets others take the lead at home. He stays out of the squabbles between his feuding wives, and his sons soon recognise a power vacuum. Given his situation, I cannot see myself doing any better. And yet it is not all doom and gloom. Somehow, Jacob finds the time and energy to give one of his sons a grounding in spiritual truth. Although he must leave his precious coat behind him en route to Egypt, Joseph takes a working faith and powerful relationship with God into the unknown. It is a remarkable tribute to his father whose true gift turns out not to be the contentious garb his young son sported.

And, against all the odds, the whole unmanageable crew finally learns to worship as Jacob lays down the law and leads the way at Bethel. Despite serious individual flaws, these people provide a base from which God can work, the soil that produces Moses, the prophets, the kings. And of course the kingdom, in time, finds an everlasting King.

Inside out

Despite all the action, something is happening inside Jacob, too. It is hard to see exactly what is going on because it does not happen quickly, nor is progress always even. However, even after recognising the setbacks and upsets, we see that the father who blesses his sons in Genesis 49 is a very different character from the schemer who lives in so much of the text. Something has happened to the man who relied so heavily on his own efforts and who levered the most out of every opportunity. To be sure, he is still playing a long game, perhaps much longer than he realised. A naïve approach to the text (and I am very naïve in such matters) has a few centuries between the blessings and their initial fulfilment (read Joshua 13-21).

But the game at the end has a different quality. No longer is Jacob driven by his forceful sons. He moves the big blessing, the firstborn's blessing, down from number one (Reuben) to number four (Judah). As a younger man, he would surely have let it slip all the way to number eleven (Joseph) – but not any more.

More than anything else, however, Jacob sees that success and failure in life are not meant to be our burden. Our job is to learn to worship and, given that, it is almost impossible to mess up. Jacob knows about messing up. He has messed up relationships at home and in Haran. He has struggled to build a flock fit to retire on and then risked it all in a senseless dash for freedom, leaving his future (not to mention his family) scattered across the hillside, wide open to the vengeful attentions of Uncle Laban and his henchmen.

And yet it has been amazingly difficult for Jacob to do any real damage to his prospects. Eventually he enjoys the blessing God had promised to his mother before he was born and that his father, unintentionally, delivered to him. The turning point, as I see it, is that Jacob slowly learns to stop trying and to start worshipping. The cadence might have been better if I had said that he learned to stop trying and started trusting. That is how we usually put it. But I'm not sure that is the message. I believe that it is only as Jacob focuses on God in personal worship, devoting to God that mental energy that he had channelled into planning, to face-offs, that determination that went into hard work, it is only then that he succeeds.

What's in it for us?

Because Jacob is such a real character – so rounded and full of life – there is a lot that he has to offer us today, some of which I may manage to capture in this book.

As a hard worker, offering no excuses but getting on with the hand dealt him, Jacob may say something to the workaholics, the self-made people – particularly men – of our own era.

As someone who desperately wants to be successful, he has something to say to a society that worships success. Incidentally, if you think this book will make you rich, you are probably wasting your time and would be better off in a different section of the bookstore. However, I hope it may help you decide what you mean by success.

As a father enmeshed in a hideously complicated set of relationships, not wholly of his own making, we may see some of our own relationships. As families collide, collocate, fracture and split, Jacob's home life becomes ever more recognisable. It is certainly more comprehensible to us than it would have been to our parents or grandparents.

As a man with a sense of the spiritual, an almost magical concept that God will bless him one day, he shares a value set with those around and may have something to say to us. As a man who struggles to fit worship into a busy schedule, he may offer something to a generation too busy to be anything other than busy.

I love Jacob

Perhaps one of the most difficult passages in Scripture is the start of Malachi. Through the prophet, God says: 'Yet I have loved Jacob, but Esau I have hated' (Mal 1:2 and 3)

That sentence takes us into territory I am not planning to explore. If the negative side of the sentiment worries you (and I can understand that it would) try digging into a commentary or two. Try to grasp what the comparison might have meant to the first hearers. If you struggle with a God who seems arbitrarily to choose between twin brothers, predestining one for blessing, you are tackling a profound aspect of Christian faith that will reward your study. How does an all-powerful God interact with fragile people possessed, of all things, by a will of their own?

I just want us to tackle the bits we can make sense of without getting bogged down with the bits we cannot. That is not to say that there are not good answers to some of the problems just raised. I believe there are and that there is great reward in setting out to find them.

However, I also believe there is great reward to addressing the simpler question: why would God prefer Jacob to Esau? I am quite sure that many of us would have gone the other way on first meeting. After all, Esau was the man who made his mark on the big wide world. Esau was the skilful hunter, an outdoor man in a millennium of outdoor people. He won the respect of the locals, several of whom were pleased to marry their daughters off to him. In other ways, too, Esau enjoys the sunnier personality, prepared to bury the hatchet with a warm welcome when he and Jacob are reunited at last.

Next to his uncomplicated brother, Jacob cuts a cramped, edgy figure on the fringe of society, a quiet man who busies himself about the tents. Before celebrity chefdom might have offered him a viable career, Jacob makes do with his lot, cooking what he cannot catch. While we admire his sheer persistence and determination, it must have been little fun to have Jacob around, storing up grievances, waiting his moment, mercilessly exploiting his advantage when the right situation finally arrived.

So why does God go for Jacob? In one sense, it comes as a pleasant surprise to discover that God is interested in such people as Jacob. If God can go for Jacob, he can go for me. No matter how unpromising my start, how introverted or irritating my personality, there is hope for me. In fact, the New Testament amplifies this theme until it becomes almost unbearable in its clarity. We do not make it with God on the basis of pleasing personality or physical perfection. God accepts that the whole human race is flawed and in Jesus he offers a route for anyone, including and often especially the worst, to enjoy his blessing.

That is a wonderful truth, but I think there is one more truth worth exploring before we start to study Jacob in a little more detail. You see, Jacob learns to worship. Esau, for all his wonderful personality and skills, never seems to get beyond himself. What little evidence there is of his spiritual outlook shows a clear antipathy to, perhaps even contempt for, his parents' God. Jacob takes a different path and, while he undertakes it clumsily and in a self-centred manner, it leads him into the presence of God.

This may not seem like a big deal to us. To God, however, there is quite literally a world of a difference. Not all attributes are equal. Some things matter much more than others. I recently started to play Hearts, one of the card games on your PC. Someone had introduced me to the game a while ago and I had a vague recollection that it was all about losing tricks – the person who had the fewest points won the game. So I started to try losing tricks. However, it is quite difficult to lose every trick and I found my score mounting and my position falling, often to last place. In the end I gave up and hit the help button to find out how the scoring works. It turns out that all tricks are not worth the same. Some tricks will cost you nothing. Actually it is only tricks with hearts that cost you – one point per heart. Unless, of course, you capture the queen of spades. For some arbitrary reason, this costs you a whacking 13 points. There is a final arbitrary twist to the scoring in which you can capture every heart plus the queen of spades in one game and escape without penalty, dumping a serious load of points on your opponents. My main discovery, then, was that one card counts for as much as all the others put together.

And worship is like that – only more so. It outweighs everything else.

And the same is true in our world. While we are not judged by the same standards as Esau in our world, we are tempted nonetheless to fulfil the expectations of those around us. The message from Jacob is that learning to worship is worth any amount of planning, scheming, hard work, or guts. At least as far as God is concerned.

Rather than working through things historically, I hope we can pick up some themes and follow them through. Chapter 1 seeks to outline Jacob's character, identifying the main features and fleshing them out. Since a lot of Jacob's journey is about success, I thought it would be worth thinking briefly about success in chapter 2. Is success a Christian concept?

Chapters 3 and 4 take a look at his spiritual journey, examining the sort of faith he had when he left home and the way in which this develops. We will look at high intensity events, such as his amazing encounters with God at Bethel, but also think about the impact of time, sometimes long stretches of time, on his faith. And we will try to understand what was important about where he ended up.

The next chapter (5) considers Jacob's relationships and the way in which he manages them. How does God help him to repair those he has broken? Chapter 6 looks at Jacob at home, Jacob as a husband, as a parent, a father and then a grandfather. And then, to pull things together in chapter 7, we take a look at Jacob from the perspective of Hebrews 11 – that chapter on faith where Jacob gets a mention. The last chapter takes a personal approach to the question of how much we should do for ourselves and how much we should trust.

Is this a book for men only? I hope not. But I hope it does speak to men. I think men find it hard to be effective Christians today and I will try to explore some of the reasons for this as we move through Jacob's story. I hope that men reading this book will realise that it has never been easy to walk with God but will be encouraged to see how rewarding it was for Jacob in the end. Could it have been written with a wider focus? Yes, but I can only give of what I am and have – and I'm a man, a husband, a father, trying to understand a great Bible character who was all of these, and much more.

However there are two reasons why I trust this material will carry a wider appeal. First, I hope this book opens up a way of looking at Jacob, rather than prescribing a set of lessons about him. To that extent, half the fun lies in getting your own take on Jacob, adapting the teaching to your perspective. Second, questions about being a good father or husband cannot be answered by men only. If this book helps to open up the issues so that Christian couples, for instance, can seek Christian models for their marriages, I will be content.

But enough of all that! Let's get on with the story.

1

God and the Dealer

As I explained in the preface, earlier on this year I was working with a team of men ranging in age from early twenties to mid fifties. We were looking for a way into Jacob's life, something that would enable the whole church to identify with him. Eventually Del Boy, the lovable wide boy from *Only Fools and Horses*, put in an appearance. A fan of the series even found a clip where Del Boy tries to flog some dodgy, early mobile phones. The phone interferes with the TV in the pub, providing an entertaining sequence, since Boycie and his mates are trying to watch the racing.

As I write, I live in Essex, home of can-do people. Essex Man in his white socks is the archetypal salesman, closing a deal on his mobile while he convinces you that your central heating system is dead and that, incidentally, his mate could do you a great conservatory while you're having the double glazing done. Essex Girl is formidable, too, taking life and her man by the scruff of the neck, singing hits, partying 'til dawn in Ibiza and generally having a great time.

We all love a deal maker, particularly one with a good sense of humour who does not rip us off too badly. And I guess that seeing Jacob as a sort of Essex Man meets Del Boy is not that far from the truth. Jacob is always looking for his next deal.

His amazing ability to spot the angle, coupled with a determination to press home his advantage when the situation is ripe, seems to offer him the only way out of a rather dull existence playing second fiddle to Esau.

Of course, God had promised his mother even before the twins were born that Jacob would be special (Gen 25:23):

The LORD said to her,
> 'Two nations are in your womb,
> and two peoples from within you will be separated;
> one people will be stronger than the other,
> and the older will serve the younger.'

But somehow it did not seem to be working out that way. Isaac had taken a shine to Esau and Esau was able to deliver the goods. He filled the table with game and got on well with the neighbours. And one day it would all belong to Esau. How do you succeed in an environment like that?

We may find ourselves in similar situations, locked into unfulfilling roles with no seeming way out. Perhaps you have lived in the shadow of an older brother or sister. Perhaps he or she has always enjoyed a better press from your parents. Maybe you have put in more work, 'among the tents'. Even now, while you work hard to make their lives easier in their old age, they extol the virtues of your absent sibling.

There are lots of ways in which we deal with this. I have just read Stefan Kanfer's biography of Groucho Marx. In it, the author attributes some of the turmoil in Groucho's life to the fact that he was never his mother's favourite – he always felt he had something to prove.

Leaving it with God

The trouble, of course, with this type of character study is that you cannot re-run the character in different phases. We might guess why Jacob's approach fails. However, the story is such a mix of principle and circumstance, that it is not easy to identify exactly what has gone wrong. What we cannot do is set the scene up again and watch Jacob take another course. We do not see the domestic difficulties addressed by a Jacob prepared to talk to God about his predicament and leave it there. However, there is a twist in this story that might point us in the right direction.

As is so often the case, although Jacob suffers from inequitable situations, he is also responsible for generating such pressures for others, and in watching Leah respond to a similar situation we get a clue as to how it might have worked out. I cannot imagine the stresses Leah underwent as the unloved wife. I am not sure how you would begin to counsel a couple arriving on your doorstep locked into that sort of relationship. It is not that Leah never bargains. In exchanging Reuben's mandrake plants (Gen 30:14-17) to buy a slot in bed with Jacob, she shows that she has not watched him all those years for nothing. However, on the whole she must endure.

And God rewards her in the long run. In a society where she

would be valued highly for the children she bore and the number of sons in particular, she gives birth to over half the family, including six of Jacob's dozen sons. And it is Leah who is buried with Jacob, in the family burial cave alongside Abraham and Sarah, and Isaac and Rebekah (Gen 49:31). These blessings may not be top of your list of priorities, but in her world, these things would have mattered.

As we considered the act-or-trust paradigm in our group, the team came up with a couple of examples in which God had worked on their behalf. A young graduate had been progressing well at work up North when he was suddenly made redundant. He needed to work and found a job at a factory, got his head down and made the best of an uninspiring role. What surprised him was that, having decided to settle at what was to hand, he received a 'phone call from a communications company he had tried earlier. He never worked out how they got his mobile number – but an offer came through with a relocation package, and he and his family were on their way. He now feels quite confident that God is able to sort things out for him, which is a great lesson to have under his belt with the uncertainties of the communications business just now.

Another chap works for himself and described his struggles, early on, in trying to keep his business going. There was no defining moment for him, but he explained that, after much agonising, he learned that he had to hand things over to God. He is not a millionaire, but God is doing what he promised in providing the daily bread, and a whole lot of worry has been taken out of the equation.

Finding a foothold

But Jacob cannot endure. Jacob may be a quiet man, but he must find a foothold and start to ascend. He is a wheeler-dealer to the core, and when his time comes, he drives his bargains hard, as we see in the way he handles the birthright (Gen 25:29-34). Esau is starving and Jacob wants the birthright. He knows they can both get what they want – Esau in the short term, Jacob in the long run. Someone as smart as Jacob must have realised that this would only wreck an already shaky relationship with Esau but presumably he does not care. He gets what he wants at considerable cost to the relationship and to his personal integrity.

We must be careful in judging Jacob by New Testament standards and, as we shall see, both his father and grandfather had taken the easy route when it came to telling the truth. And let's not forget that Jacob must have known of God's promise to Rebekah. He shows all the signs of someone in hot pursuit of what is rightfully his.

Perhaps that makes it easier to deceive his father, Isaac, in order to get the firstborn's blessing (Gen 27). In a situation requiring steady nerves and quick thinking, and where failure would have been absolute, Jacob shows us what a cool operator he is. Everything he has waited and hoped for is about to go down the tube. Granted, his mother plays a key role in putting him up to it, but Jacob is not going to sit around and let his dream drift into his brother's lap. The plan is desperate, but he makes the best of it and carries it through.

His bargaining position is really weak when, weeks or months later, he rolls up at Uncle Laban's (Gen 29-31). After the preliminaries are over, there is the sticky problem of what to do with this unemployed nephew. Given the culture and the family ties, the solution is natural enough, but it may have been a hard pill to swallow for the ambitious Jacob. Perhaps life at home with the run of the tents as long as his father was still alive seemed suddenly very attractive.

But Jacob is the supreme realist. He tightens his links by marrying into the family (as, indeed, his father had specified) and accepts the incredible indignity of waking up with the wrong bride. However awkward and unpromising his position, he knuckles down to the humble task of looking after someone else's flocks. He will build his herd from the less favoured animals. But his key strategy for this period of his life is sheer hard work and numbingly long hours, as he makes clear in that famous, final, blow-up with Laban (Gen 31:38-42). Not that this prevents him from using some fairly dubious methods as well, such as mating the best sheep in front of stripy poles in order to get the colour scheme that he has agreed with Laban will be his share of the flock at the time (Gen 30:37-43).

Having said all this, it is worth noting that Jacob takes a high moral view of his actions. For instance, in negotiating his wages with Laban, he says (Gen 30:32 and 33): 'Let me go through all your flocks today and remove from them every speckled or spotted sheep, every dark-colored lamb and every spotted or speckled goat. They will be my wages. And my honesty will testify for me in the future, whenever you check on the wages you have paid me. Any goat in my possession that is not speckled or spotted, or any lamb that is not dark-colored, will be considered stolen.' You sometimes get people who will do this. And you can find lots of examples of Christians having this sort of double take integrity – attention to detail on the one hand, huge moral question marks on the other. You may find the Christian couple letting a holiday cottage who have a watertight contract, but omit to tell you that your car parking space is 200 steps down a cliff face. Or perhaps there is the Christian lender who sticks mercilessly to the terms.

My guess is, that the higher a view we take of our personal integrity, the easier it is to fall into the trap of behaving disingenuously outside the narrow confines of the rules we set ourselves. I am not suggesting we adopt a lower standard of personal integrity – merely that we need more humility in applying it. We may also need more faith to seek a broader integrity. All in all, I am not sure that Jacob's integrity is any poorer than that of the average Christian today. I certainly recognise a great deal of myself in him.

And me?

As I was working with the team to bring out some of these themes, I was aware of two sensations. The first was that slightly uneasy feeling you sometimes get when you think God may have something to say to you. At the time, I was still going through a difficult patch at work. At a time of change, I was being asked to take up a role with which I felt I would be profoundly unhappy. I found myself applying every piece of negotiating skill I had, trying to find those angles, those footholds that would give me some bargaining leverage toward a solution I would find more acceptable. And on Monday evenings, we were talking about trusting God and not trying to do it all yourself. My fear was that maybe God was asking me to swallow my pride and leave the rest to him.

My second feeling was that Jacob might have something interesting to say to my situation. It is always a little more fun to study scripture when the application is obvious, and I found myself getting very interested from a personal viewpoint.

Most of us have a little of the Del Boy about us. We struggle for a foothold, look for a better deal, desperately trying to better our lot. Sometimes it is just a game. If you enjoy negotiating, everything is a search for a deal. In the early '90s my wife and I had a small windfall and decided to buy a sitting room suite. We trudged around the furniture stores, searching for a good deal. At one stage we saw a really nice three-seat bed settee by a well-known brand. Sadly, I decided to bargain for it. In the end, they didn't like my offer and we walked away. We found a small furniture maker who would make us a suite with a chaise longue – something I fancied – and Dani has hated the suite ever since. I just love to get a discount. Dani sneaks off once we have chosen something to be well away by the time the bargaining begins. Although I enjoy the thrill of the chase, I am not a great dealer. I am surrounded by people who can get 25% off, to my 10%. I remember bargaining a bed down, only to see the same model at almost the same price in a sale later on that summer. One of my brothers once described to me how he had negotiated for the car he was driving – and I realised how much ground I have to make up if I am to excel in the field.

But sometimes the bargain is more than a good deal. How will we keep the mortgage payments up without that next promotion? How will we miss the drop in the next round of redundancies? How will we get out of the rut we are in? How will we ever escape from that manager we hate? Does it matter how we go about it, so long as our team wins the bid?

Incidentally, in the end I gave up the struggle at work. I opted for a severance package and found, as Jacob discovered eventually, that it is very hard to go wrong.

Dealing with God

I suppose we should not be surprised to find Jacob adopting the same approach with God. Remember his first real, personal encounter with God? It is after he has fled the nest (Gen 28:10-22). God meets him in a dream and makes the most astounding promises to him, reinforcing the prophecy to his mother and his father's blessing. Look at the scope and quality of the promise.

What is Jacob's reaction? First of all, he is clearly shaken and awed – a promising start. When we come to plot Jacob's journey of faith in chapter 3, we will see that this marks a big step forward in Jacob's relationship.

But his second reaction is to try to pull some sort of bargaining position out of the encounter. He wants to deal with God – 'if... then' (Gen 28:20-22). He has nothing to offer, nothing to put on the table except the promise that God has just given him, and a tenth of the wealth he has yet to acquire. And still he wants to do a deal. We may admire him for his guts, but I suspect most of us are stunned by his cheek.

Later on in life, isolated and alone once more, we find him again wrestling with a stranger (Gen 32:24-31). Again he senses there is a deal to be done. Jacob is still thirsting for that blessing and even when he cannot win, he will not let go. What is it Kipling says?

> If you can force your heart and nerve and sinew
> To serve their turn long after they are gone,
> And so hold on when there is nothing in you
> Except the Will which says to them: 'Hold on!'

And so Jacob holds on, determined to wring another blessing from the situation.

The great thing to notice here is that Jacob is a real person. He is not a saint at church and a shark in the workplace. It is perhaps surprising that someone as shrewd and switched on as Jacob should fail to take a more circumspect approach to God. And yet it shows how deeply our traits are ingrained. What is obvious when we look at others is not always visible when we look at ourselves. Our greatest strengths are also our greatest weaknesses – the penguin's wings that work so well under water are a waste of space on the ice.

Dealing with Jacob

So how does God deal with Jacob? If Jacob's approach to God is surprising, God's ways with Jacob are a real shock.

Let's stand back for a moment. God wants to bless Jacob. At every opportunity, God is unswerving in his commitment to bless Jacob. The same promises made to his father and grandfather, are made, once more, to Jacob. But the only way God can really bless Jacob is through a working relationship where Jacob gets to know God, to understand what God really wants, to feel the tick of God's heart.

Now suppose that you were the angel to whom God had

assigned Jacob. Suppose it were your task to bring Jacob through all his difficulties to a place where he could have a working relationship with God. How would you go about it? If you are an educationalist, or if you are into behavioural psychology, you will have great fun with this question. I have only the most basic view of this but as I understand it, there are two main approaches. Either you punish people for getting things wrong and reward them for getting things right, or you try to reward people from the start, believing that they will feel better about themselves and go on towards improved behaviour. The former approach tends to lay a heavy accent on the penalty of getting things wrong. It leads to workhouses, to prisons, but also to honours and social advancement. The other approach sees young offenders sent on outdoor pursuit holidays. It does not seem to me that Jacob's experience follows either path.

I am not proposing here to dive into a question of social justice. I believe God is entirely just and merciful in dealing with Jacob. What I want to try and follow is where God meets Jacob and how Jacob is led on from there.

If Jacob is like most of us, he will attribute his successes to the things he has done – and has presumably gotten right. He may attribute some of his failures to poor decisions, although like most of us, he seems to focus less on his failures than his grievances as we see, for instance, in his argument with his uncle, Laban (Gen 31:25-42).

So what would you do? Would you withhold all blessing until Jacob realises that his scheming, wheeler-dealing approach to life is wrong? Would you bless him at the risk of his misinterpreting it as a response to the bargain he has struck?

To me, the surprising thing is that God does not seem to be put off by Jacob's attempts to strike a deal. God does not respond to Jacob in the desert by telling him to get lost if he cannot accept the promise, gratis. God's unswerving purpose is to bless Jacob and, although Jacob's decisions make it difficult to fulfil that plan and often set it back a long way, Jacob emerges from each scenario better off than he entered it.

In a strange way, we have to remember that God is God and cannot be blackmailed by Jacob's attempts to turn every blessing into a bargain. I wonder sometimes whether we really understand how deeply God wants to bless each of his children. Of course, we also need to understand the nature of that blessing and think a bit about what we mean by success, but there will be time for that in the next chapter.

So God meets Jacob where he is. God actually fulfils the 'if' side of Jacob's bargain, and brings him home safely. Years later, the stranger blesses Jacob and gives him a new name. In the most perplexing move of all, Laban's ewes bear spotty lambs, stripy lambs, or whatever colour lambs Jacob needs at the time, despite his chicanery at mating time (Gen 30:37-43 and Gen 31:10-13).

I think there is an important message here for all of us. We try something and God blesses us, so we tell other people that they have to do the same thing in the same way. Sometimes we have hit upon a spiritual truth and others would benefit from following our lead. Sometimes, we have taken the germ of a truth well beyond the purpose for which it was intended and still God has blessed us. Perhaps we have learned to pray in a particular way. Maybe we have a specific sequence of ideas, maybe we have a particular style of meditation, maybe our church has developed a particular style of evangelism – and God is blessing. Well praise God! God is doing for you or your church what he desperately wants to do in bringing blessing. But blessing is not a rubber stamp on our methods.

Maybe I have run a tight ship at work and we have beaten our targets. Maybe my bonus is up this year. Maybe I have been promoted three times in the past two years. Maybe I have been told that I am particularly highly valued as the next round of redundancies looms. Maybe I have finally found a boss whom I really like and who really likes the way I do things. Maybe I have a job that really stretches and fulfils me. Maybe the children have started to excel at school. Maybe I have the kitchen I longed for. Maybe we have just bought the retirement bungalow we have always dreamed of. Does any of this mean that God is satisfied with my life or that my methods are spot on? If we look to Jacob, we might have to say, not necessarily.

Staving off disaster

That is not to say that God has granted Jacob a life of luxury. We have noted the grinding passage of the years. Part of the way in which God changes Jacob is the way he changes all of us – by allowing us to get older. Jacob has plenty of the down side of his decisions and, although blessed in the end, he has to sweat and tear his way through many decades before he enjoys the real blessing of prosperity with peace.

But God does something else for Jacob in protecting him when his behaviour could have cost him his life. When an enraged Laban sets out to overhaul his nephew and bring his relative and associated property back inside the fold, God warns Laban that he is to do him no harm (Gen 31:24). This strengthens Jacob's hand immeasurably in the ensuing engagement, since it appears that Jacob would have been seriously outnumbered in any conflict.

Again, in the tragic story of Dinah and the Shechemites (Gen 34), Jacob realises that he is extremely vulnerable, should the neighbouring sheiks decide that Simeon and Levi were well out of order in the revenge they extracted for their sister's rape, despite the fact that Jacob seems to be a significant presence with a large supporting cast of servants (e.g. Gen 30:43). But we read that God made the surrounding towns terrified of this nomad and the family proceeds safely (Gen 35:5).

I wonder how many times I have done something really crass and God has worked in the background to ensure that I have not borne the full consequences of my stupidity, opening up an unexpected opportunity, creating a bolt-hole, saving my skin? Given my capacity for messing things up, I am sure it has happened, but I have no good example to offer you. Perhaps you could ask around and find your own example.

Dealing with the dealer

So God meets Jacob the dealer, the shyster, the hustler, and God is prepared to start where he, Jacob, is. If Jacob wants deals, God will not demur, but neither will he be deflected from his purposes in Jacob's life. In a slightly different take, David says (2 Sam 22:27 and Psalm 18:26):

> To the pure you show yourself pure,
>   but to the crooked you show yourself shrewd.

And that is one of the great things about God. He starts with us as we are. God does not ask me to become a completely different person before I can come to him. He asks me to come in order that I might become – a different person. As time goes on, we see the flaws in Jacob emerging as strengths. In time, his ability to read a situation enables him to see with clarity what is really happening in his own family. In time, he finds that he can really wrestle with God and be commended for the endeavour. In time, his sheer rugged determination enables him to cross the desert as a very, very old man, to meet Joseph once more. In time, all those skills of being able to size someone up, of reading body language, of engaging in delicate negotiations, all those skills are invested in a rewarding relationship with God. But not just yet.

The long game

I hope you are beginning to recognise the sort of character Jacob was – the skilful planner, the shrewd evaluator, the schemer, the dealer. I hope you appreciate something of his determination so that, while he will not fight battles he believes he cannot win, given the right vantage point, he will press his case ruthlessly. But we cannot do justice to Jacob as a person without recognising one more strength – his patience.

Esau was a hunter and lived from day to day. That is what hunters do. If they fail in the hunt, they go hungry for a while – or they do sad deals with their more prudent brothers. If they lose their grip on the bow, they starve unless they have the offspring to keep things going. Jacob is not quite a farmer, dependent as he is on the swing of the seasons and continually trekking after the greenery. But he is naturally inclined to a longer term game than Esau.

It comes out in his career. It emerges in his dealings with Esau where he waits for his opportunities. It comes out in his dealing with Laban, where he accepts the raw disappointment and humiliation of having Leah foisted upon him to play the longer game – Rachel! Given the option of paying another seven years (this time in arrears), he enters a second work-for-wife agreement. Jacob will let an indignity pass and deal with it when he gets the leverage to do the matter justice – and until then he will wait. Leaving home without any possessions, he patiently builds his herd until he has wealth to amaze even wealthy Esau. And so Jacob's story is spread out over decades.

Perhaps Jacob's patience is linked a little to fear. Perhaps he fears Laban's ire. There are times when we know Jacob is concerned about the opposition, whether it be allusions to Laban's

sons (Gen 31:1) or to the people around (Gen 34:30). Yet Jacob is
no weakling. Presumably, he removes the well cover on his own
(Gen 29:10), knowing that this is a break with tradition. Later on,
we see his ability to survive harsh nights with Laban's flock. But
sometimes there is something in there that sticks clear of a fight.
Jacob will dig in and hang on for his rights, but he does not push
people around. If anything, he has a knack of sparking off fights
by trying to run away from them.

And so we round off our picture of Jacob, with his guile and
dealing skills. Although he becomes a muscular character, he
generally chooses the prudent path, even if it takes longer,
avoiding open conflict where possible. Despite feeling that he
has a strong moral code, he is prepared to deceive, even within
the family circle. Beyond all this, Jacob knows what he wants
and is absolutely determined to go after it.

Jacob is after the blessing.

Thinking it through

1. You are progressing well in bringing down the price on the
   house on which you are planning to make an offer, when
   you discover the seller is a Christian. Does this affect the
   deal? If it does, how? Should it?

2. Think of two characteristics that have helped make you
   successful. To what extent do they need to be redeemed?
   What will they look like when God has finished with
   them?

3. A new programme of redundancies is about to be
   implemented and your boss suggests you find an opening
   in another part of the company. What steps would you
   take, at work, at home and at church?

4. You discover that a colleague at work, who, you thought,
   was backing you for the new position, has applied and
   secured the position herself. What is your reaction?

5. Your non-Christian boss accuses you of twisting the facts to
   win an argument. How do you respond – at the time, and
   later?

6. Your new boss is a young chap who wants you to be one of
   the lads. As time progresses you feel increasingly
   uncomfortable with his approach to doing business. How

would Jacob have advised you when he was a young man? How about when he was an old man?

7. List three ways in which God has blessed you. How much of this was due to your own efforts?

8. When should Christians be opportunistic?

9. Can a good salesman be a good Christian? Explain your answer.

2

Success!

The great paradox in Jacob's story is that God wants to give Jacob what Jacob wants to get – the blessing! But God's idea of blessing and Jacob's idea are not well aligned, and much of the narrative is devoted to a struggle as Jacob attempts to grab his idea of a blessing while God plays a patient game to bring Jacob to a point where he can really enjoy the blessing God has been lining up all along.

So what is Jacob after in life? Jacob wants land and property. While he probably wants descendants as much as anyone in his society would, it is not clear that he has the same driving ambition for children as for possessions. Sure, he bargains for a wife, in fact for two wives, before he bargains for flocks and herds. But both the birthright and his father's blessing (Gen 27:27-29) are much more focused on possessions and status.

And if your grandfather had upped sticks and moved beyond the frontier with a promise of blessing in a land his descendants would one day own, you might want the same. If your father and your grandfather had both wandered in a land that neither had come to own, you might share their aspirations but also feel that maybe it was time for the family to take hold of its potential and realise the assets latent in the promises. The sense that the land is theirs is one of the most deeply ingrained and unifying features in Israel today.

It must have been a hazardous existence following the rains, fighting with local sheiks and landowners over wells, never far from extinction in the next savage raid. Perhaps if we remembered how precarious it all was, we would be kinder to Abraham and Isaac as they turn a blind eye when the local potentate decides to incorporate their wives into his harem. But getting back to Jacob, what is the use of such a promise if so much of your life is lived just a whisker away from disaster? Would not the blessing, with its rich promises, make life a great deal more secure if only it could be invoked in Jacob's lifetime?

Security through possessions. I think Jacob's concept of the blessing comes quite close to what most men today would think of as success.

But what is God's concept here? Surprisingly, in one sense, God's aim is not that far away from Jacob's aspiration. Certainly, God wants Jacob to be secure. As we shall see, wave after wave of promises and blessings can only be intended to reassure Jacob and help him to realise that it will be all right in the end. Insecurity is one of the great burdens people face and Jesus devotes swathes of teaching to it (e.g. Luke 12:11-34).

But security through what? As I understand it, God offers security through relationship, a relationship with God mediated by Jesus. That is why so many of the New Testament blessings come, 'in Christ'. It is why Paul writes to his friends in Corinth: 'For no matter how many promises God has made, they are "Yes" in Christ' (2 Cor 1:20).

If our concept of success has not changed markedly since Jacob's time, God's aims have remained similarly constant, and we may well find ourselves facing the same frustrations and struggles that characterised Jacob's life.

Success in the real world

Ah yes. We all know how it should work in theory, but I have to live in the real world. I have to struggle to find a job that will keep my family. I need worry about a pension to prepare me for a world where I might live to be 108, where my grandchildren may have reached what I would consider retirement age before I die. I need some protection against my pension fund failing, my portfolio crashing, a spell of unemployment, or a dive in the house market given my mortgage exposure.

And while I am at it, I don't see why I should not do as well as my neighbour who is a financial adviser or my boss who has never really worked out how to get the best from our team. I work harder than either, why should I not enjoy the benefits? Why should I not park a new car on the drive?

Why should I not moor a boat on the river? Why should my friends not respect me for the way I have succeeded at work? Surely, so long as I have not cheated or stolen to get what I have, so long as I give generously, surely it is fine to keep and to build.

And anyway, despite all this spiritual analysis, God shows his favour to Jacob through material blessings. Perhaps this is just a case of first and second things, as C S Lewis called it. He talked about things you do not get until you go after something else. Perhaps material success is like that. Perhaps God wants to pile material goodies on his children but only if they are not really after them. After all, that is what happens, particularly in the Old Testament, to so many of God's people. Joseph learns to walk with God as a slave and then as a prisoner and is elevated to Prime Minister. Moses builds a relationship with God over four decades in the back of beyond and comes back as founding ruler of the nation. Caleb displays his faith and receives Hebron as his inheritance (Joshua 14:13). David learns to worship and gains the kingdom.

It is not hard to build a theology around this, teaching that God wants his children to be well off – the healthy, wealthy and wise theology. The protestant work ethic may come from a slightly different perspective but drives us in a similar direction. In this model of Christian success, Christians seek God, work hard, and God rewards them with material prosperity.

Wealth

Apart from the obvious question of how we can truly seek after God when we expect to be rewarded in such a direct and obvious way, it is worth asking whether this view is true. It may appeal to those of us who live in Europe or North America where there is political stability, where Christianity is broadly tolerated, and where there are plenty of opportunities for hardworking talented people. But does it work in other frameworks where the church has less of a positive profile, where Christianity is unpopular, or where Christians might face discrimination or even persecution? Do Christians form a wealthy middle-class fringe in those parts of the world?

Some see the Old Testament as providing models, which are somehow spiritualised in the New. And sometimes this approach works. The sacrificial system clearly gives way to a once-for-all sacrifice and Christians rightly see the imagery of daily sacrifices in terms, for instance, of worship and prayers ascending like the smoke to God. Perhaps physical blessings, too, give way to spiritual blessings.

But even this oversimplifies the Old Testament teaching on wealth and success. I always think Proverbs is a great place to go for ideas on money. After all, Solomon had plenty of it – but more of that later. How do you read Proverbs? I found it hard because the writer always seems to be dodging about all over the place. I think it is probably because that type of writing is quite hard to grapple with. One thing you can do with Proverbs, however, is to string the verses on similar topics together. With our laptops and Bibles on CD, it is a trivial exercise to skim and trace various themes through. When you do that, the necklace you get has lustre and pattern.

So what insights does the book of Proverbs provide into wealth? I will not pick up all the references, but here is some of the teaching. First, wealth can, indeed, provide that security we have talked about, and it can be a blessing from God:

The wealth of the rich is their fortified city,
    but poverty is the ruin of the poor (Prov 10:15).

The blessing of the LORD brings wealth,
    and he adds no trouble to it (Prov 10:22).

The wealth of the rich is their fortified city;
    they imagine it an unscalable wall (Prov 18:11).

However, it is not as simple as that:

Wealth is worthless in the day of wrath,
    but righteousness delivers from death (Prov 11:4).

A kindhearted woman gains respect,
    but ruthless men gain only wealth (Prov 11:16).

Better a little with the fear of the LORD
    than great wealth with turmoil (Prov 15:16).

And in Solomon himself, despite his amazing insights, we find a man who could not master the competition between a love of God and other loves. The Old Testament Law was very clear (Deut 17:16 and 17): 'The king, moreover, must not acquire great numbers of horses for himself or make the people return to Egypt to get more of them, for the LORD has told you, "You are not to go back that way again." He must not take many wives, or his heart will be led astray. He must not accumulate large amounts of silver and gold.' Solomon broke every piece of advice given here. Although his wives are cited as the prime reason for his downfall in drawing him towards other gods, his amazing affluence was what provided him with the means to maintain such an extensive harem.

Jesus put it very simply (Matt 6:24): 'You cannot serve both God and Money.' Not only is Solomon the wealthiest king Israel ever had, not only does he reign over a kingdom that stretches further than it has done since, but it can hardly be a coincidence that he is also the king who precipitates the sad decline that ended ultimately in exile. I appreciate the role that idolatry played in Israel's downfall, but it is hard to read Isaiah (e.g. Isa 3:16) and the other prophets (e.g. Amos 8:1-7, Zeph 1:7-13) without catching the raw end of God's anger against the arrogance that goes with affluence and the desire to amass wealth. Many people today will note that a desire to be wealthy, as well as creating an inevitable competitor in our affections for God, has a side effect in the way it distorts society. Social justice is a whole new topic but does not, as I see it, impact on much of Jacob's story – although it would be a fun topic for another book!

I believe the Old Testament promotes a mixed view of wealth. It is commended where honestly and diligently obtained and God's hand is recognised in bestowing it. On the other hand, the pursuit of wealth as an end in itself is increasingly reviled, particularly as you move into the Prophets, and it is presented as an ineffective source of security.

If anything, the New Testament warnings related to wealth are more direct and dire than in the Old. We have Jesus' own words (Luke 6:24 and 25):

But woe to you who are rich,
    for you have already received your comfort.

Woe to you who are well fed now,
    for you will go hungry.

Paul's letters to Timothy are practical and hardly endorse an affluent lifestyle (1 Tim 6:10, 17 and 18): 'For the love of money is a root of all kinds of evil. Some people, eager for money, have wandered from the faith and pierced themselves with many griefs... Command those who are rich in this present world not to be arrogant nor to put their hope in wealth, which is so uncertain, but to put their hope in God, who richly provides us with everything for our enjoyment. Command them to do good, to be rich in good deeds, and to be generous and willing to share.' James is even more scathing in places (e.g. Jas 5:1-6). Against this is the commendation of generosity and the role rich people played in Jesus' life and in the early church.

Getting the balance right is difficult. It seems to me that God's prime desire is to bless me, but I cannot see that he wants to make me rich. If he does so, it seems to me that he also places responsibilities on me to be generous and to share.

But whereas there are widespread tensions over personal wealth in scripture, the Bible is uniformly in favour of personal peace and contentment. God does want me to be secure! We have Jesus' own words (John 14:27): 'Peace I leave with you; my peace I give you. I do not give to you as the world gives. Do not let your hearts be troubled and do not be afraid.' Joy and peace, products of a secure life, are listed in that famous passage on the fruit of the Spirit (Gal 5:22).

Paul writes (Phil 4:12 and 13): 'I know what it is to be in need, and I know what it is to have plenty. I have learned the secret of being content in any and every situation, whether well fed or hungry, whether living in plenty or in want. I can do everything through him who gives me strength.' Hebrews contains the advice (Heb 13:5): 'Keep your lives free from the love of money and be content with what you have, because God has said,

Never will I leave you;
never will I forsake you.

In the real world

So where does this leave us in the real world? Is it wrong to be ambitious? How should I handle the annual pay negotiations? Should I ever strike out for a better job? What happens when it all works well, when my bonus overflows or the business I have just set up starts to blossom? Do I have to readjust my ideas of success? Can I ever aspire to success in its more traditional forms? How will I ever know if I have succeeded in life and am following the path God has for me?

Well, let's return to God's idea of security – security through relationship. The relationship, of course, is that we become God's children and that it is the parent-child relationship through which all blessings come. If we could really grasp what this means, if we could thoroughly understand it, it would completely change our approach to life. It becomes obvious why a life of unmitigated goodies is not what God wants for us. No truly loving parent would bring up his or her child on an exclusive diet of treats, presents, and expensive surprises.

Other things become clearer, too. The whole business of

prayer becomes really simple if we see it as part of that relationship. At the end of the day, God wants what is best for us
and gives us good things. It is certainly where the Lord's Prayer
starts – 'Our Father'. So often our approach to prayer is to try to
wrench an answer, to put in so much sincerity, effort, visualisa-
tion even, that God must respond. My children ask, and ask
again, because they are as persistent as any other child, and
asking is one of the things children are good at. They do not
worry what will happen if I say no. Sometimes they expect me
to say no.

And what do I want for my children? I want them to be
secure. I want them to be able to do things safely, to operate as
independently as they reasonably can, to be able to face new situations, to meet new people, all with confidence. Sometimes
this means taking them places where they might be a little
scared – such as that first dip in the swimming pool before they
realised how useful armbands were. Sometimes it means a modest level of pocket money so that they learn how to budget.
Sometimes it means extravagance so that they can learn generosity. But I want them to be secure.

And, generally speaking, this seems to be what success is for
a Christian: to live life in a secure relationship with his or her
Father in heaven, looking back with contentment, looking forward with confidence and being at peace in the present. If that
sounds too tranquil and passive, I have used the wrong words,
because you may be doing lots of things. Underneath, however,
I believe we should feel secure in the hands of our Heavenly
Father.

And the whole story of Jacob, as I read it, is a journey that
starts with an ambitious young man who wants materialistic
prosperity and finds security in his relationship with God.

Ambition

So should Christians be ambitious? I have struggled with this
one. At times the only way to resolve it seemed to be to divide
life into two compartments: a working compartment where you
did your best, worked your hardest and took your chances; and
a spiritual compartment where you took a more relaxed view of
life and could, perhaps, be a slightly nicer person. I think many
Christian men try that route. It does not work.

The final answer probably goes something like this. When I became a Christian, I lost all rights to my own life and there is therefore no place for ambition: 'Do you not know that your body is a temple of the Holy Spirit, who is in you, whom you have received from God? You are not your own; you were bought at a price. Therefore honor God with your body' (1 Cor 6:19 and 20).

I am not sure that this fully resolves the difficulties of how we handle our desires to excel or to do well. Do we just suppress them? Do we ask God to convert them into ambitions within his kingdom? Another problem is, quite frankly, that such teaching is pretty difficult for most men to take on board.

Again the parent-child relationship comes to our rescue. Children can always ask in confidence. Not confident of yes, but confident of the right answer. Few parents steer their offspring towards the least rewarding careers they can. They themselves may have lacked the opportunities to direct their children towards the absolute best, but they will not direct them badly. This, surely is the obvious lesson of Jesus' 'ask, seek, knock' teaching (Matt 7:7-12). Most parents will support their children as they try for that demanding interview, attempt that tricky rock face, or compete in that draining marathon.

I am just reading a biography of Brunel, the chap responsible for railways from London to Bristol, suspension bridges, tunnels and iron steamships. As a young man, it is clear that he struggles with personal ambition and is not sure what to do with it. Clearly he has vision, talent and, in time, the resources to exploit these in ambitious engineering projects. But he feels the weight of ambition and senses that it is wrong to want what he wants. He confides candidly to his diary, but beyond the catharsis this offers, he is unsure of the way ahead and ultimately he is driven to achieve his dreams. I feel the same sort of things can occur in a Christian. If I am a wonderful musician, is it wrong to want to bring music to lots of people? If I can entrance a crowd, is it wrong to seek a role in the public eye? I cannot answer those questions for you, although I am sure that simply suppressing them is hardly likely to prove the answer. In the Father-child model, we can take these things back to God. We may end up giving them up. Wellington burned his violin when he decided to become a career soldier. He felt it was necessary to put other loves out of the way in taking the path he had chosen. It is not always that straightforward, but it seems to me that we will never solve these problems by wrestling with ourselves, by trying to create scenarios in which our personal success brings or detracts from the glory of God. Best be a child and take it to Father. Let him decide.

And provided we are secure in our relationship, it seems it is difficult to ask amiss. Surely God is able to steer us away from that managing directorship if he wants to. God has a million ways of taking the edge off our ambition, as we shall see with Jacob. Sometimes it is called middle age; sometimes he brings what at first sight looks like a catastrophe; sometimes we have a nasty experience in the rat race. It would be nice to get it right from the start with all the right motives. Jacob's story seems to indicate that, even when we start at the wrong end, God can still bring us round. The only thing that prevents God from doing this is if the relationship goes. If the relationship is not there, there is no steer on our energies, no constraint to our horizon, no vision in our outlook. And that is what God begins with where Jacob is concerned. Jacob can only be secure once he has learned to worship.

As you will know, I am just at the stage where I am at a cross-roads. At the time of writing I am going after a university chair. Most people would regard that as very ambitious. I think it will be fun if I get it (and I am not just trying to put a gloss on raw ambition). I am also sure that my Heavenly Father can put a stop to it if it is the wrong thing, and there will be something else that will keep us going if this job falls through.

Within the relationship with our Father God there is clearly room for talking about money and needs. The Lord's Prayer contains the request for daily bread. Paul advises his friends in Philippi: 'Do not be anxious about anything, but in everything, by prayer and petition, with thanksgiving, present your requests to God' (Phil 4:6). Jabez (1 Chron 4:9 and 10) prays a very practical and direct prayer and gets the blessing he asks for!

Worry

I could write screeds on how to worry. In fact it seems to me that most of our messages would be more relevant and enlightening if we approached them that way. So often the sterile admonitions not to do this or that are wholly detached from any real application of teaching to the need in our lives. Perhaps that is why C S Lewis' *Screwtape Letters* works so well. Anyhow, off the hobby horse. It seems to me that fear of the future drives many men to acquire far more than they ever need – usually far more than they actually get around to spending. I like the will that went, 'I, Joe Bloggs, being of sound mind... spent it!'

But there is a message here about worry. Security has no room for worry, and if the security comes from a relationship, there is no room for worry there, either. That is why 'perfect love drives out fear' (1 John 4:18). I believe it is here, particularly, that there is challenge for us as men in a very uncertain world to claim our birthright and enjoy the benefits of a successful life.

And just now I am learning not to worry. Between jobs I am unemployed. Many of the benefits of having a pension on the go are, for a couple of months, in abeyance. I do not know where we will be living by Christmas. We do not know what schools our boys will be at. I am not perfect in this area. But I am learning. And I am not nearly as scared as I thought I would be. Sometimes I even enjoy that sense of peace I was made for. In the meantime, I am having fun writing this book.

What happened to denying yourself?

You may feel that this is a very irresponsible and self-indulgent view of success in the Christian life. What about the millions of Christians whose lot has been to suffer and be discriminated against? Did Jesus not tell us to take up our cross and follow (Matt 16:24 and 25)?

There are just two responses I would make to this – first that freedom from worry is still what Jesus bequeaths his children in their hour of trial, and second, that I cannot offer you much by way of examples of freedom from worry at the time of trial because, as yet, I have not been persecuted because of my faith.

What is Jesus' injunction to his disciples in parlous times? 'Be on your guard against men; they will hand you over to the local councils and flog you in their synagogues. On my account you will be brought before governors and kings as witnesses to them and to the Gentiles. But when they arrest you, do not worry about what to say or how to say it. At that time you will be given what to say, for it will not be you speaking, but the Spirit of your Father speaking through you' (Matt 10:17-20). Did you catch those words in the middle – 'do not worry'?

While I find it hard to imagine myself actually fulfilling that command, there is plenty of evidence in scripture that those who encountered persecution were given, as promised, that sense of peace.

My experience has not been one of persecution. I cannot write of the joy that goes with sorrow. But if I were able to do so, I think I would still write that a sense of peace and security brought about through a relationship with God is the surest measure of success in our lives.

While the bigger danger for Christians in the economically developed world is almost certainly personal enrichment at the expense of personal relationship, there is also a danger for those who really want to follow Jesus and are prepared to give everything away in pursuit of that relationship. The danger, I believe, is that they do not fully enter into the security. They lose the ability to enjoy good things when they come along. They can become very intense in their sacrifice and may lose the joy side of the security. But that temptation, as I say, is for a very small minority in the world in which I write.

And what of sacrifice? Well, it is there in scripture. Jacob's story does not cover much about sacrifice, although I am sure that as you learn to worship, you will encounter both the need for, and the blessings that go with it.

So what is success? Learn to worship and do what you like.

Thinking it through

1. How would your friends define success? In practical terms, how have you shown that you are after different things in life?

2. What would the young Jacob be after in today's society?

3. How would you account for the fact that many Christians in the UK are relatively well off while their brothers and sisters in other parts of the world have few possessions? What ideas of success could the two communities hold in common?

4. To what passages would you appeal to defend a 'healthy, wealthy and wise' definition of success for a Christian?

5. What are the dangers of refusing any material blessings

and living a Spartan lifestyle? What are the benefits?

6. List three ways in which you can show your children what counts for you as success in life.

7. What did you really believe was God's will for your life ten years ago? How did you follow it up? How have your ideas changed in the meantime?

8. List five ways in which your friends are trying to make their lives secure.

9. Think about the ways in which you are finding security. List the three that cost you most money and the three that take most time.

10. Which old person would you most want to end up like? Why?

3

The Journey Out

It may be a little dodgy to see a nomad's spiritual development in terms of a journey. While aimless meandering, following the grass, may characterise many of our lives, we may not be sure that it is a model for us to emulate. In this respect, however, Jacob's life seems more purposeful than most. He travels to destinations. He flees for his wife, he returns home. He goes to Egypt. More significantly, there is a big loop in his life as he takes a couple of decades to come back to Bethel.

If we keep an eye on Jacob, we notice that, not only is he more purposeful in his travels than many nomads, but there is a clear development in his spiritual outlook. Jacob moves on. He picks up experiences and skills en route and by the end of his life he is a very different character. My hope is that we might have a chance to examine the insights, experiences and spiritual skills he develops and see how they fit in our own life. Clearly, the order in which we learn truth as disciples will not follow Jacob's path completely. However, we may be encouraged to discover that the perplexing, unnerving experiences that Jacob underwent are not unique. Alternatively, we may discover that vital areas in Jacob's development are still virgin territory for us and it may encourage us to seek God in a new way.

Spiritually speaking, then, where does he start? Clearly, he starts in a family that fears God. God communicates with both his father and mother. In their world, their relationship with God is unique. So what is Jacob's relationship with God?

Magic!

It seems to me that Jacob's view of God is dominated by his desire to have the blessing. The blessing! Land, cattle, prosperity as his share in the patriarchal success, not to mention succession. This view, together with Jacob's drive to engineer his own success, leaves me guessing that Jacob had an almost magical view of God. If the blessing was a bit like one of Tolkein's rings, conferring status and power on the wearer, maybe he sees God as a magical force to help him get it.

Jacob seems to feel no moral responsibility towards God and yet has this deep-down belief that God is on his side. We see this, particularly in his argument with Laban at the final face-off: 'If the God of my father, the God of Abraham and the Fear of Isaac, had not been with me, you would surely have sent me away empty-handed. But God has seen my hardship and the toil of my hands, and last night he rebuked you' (Gen 31:42).

This year's tennis championships at Wimbledon provided a powerful example of the motivational force of such a belief. Goran Ivanisevic believed that this was his year and that God was on his side. He played a stunning tournament, overcoming obstacles and recovering from setbacks to win match after match and, ultimately, to lift the trophy. But it was the interviews, even before he had won the semi-finals, which were so unusual as he explained that he was going to win. It was not simply an outsider talking up his chances. Even hard-bitten journalists were astonished at the way his conviction that God was on his side and that he would win, had carried him over every barrier and on to triumph.

It certainly gives Jacob the confidence to contest both the birthright and the blessing and, in his own way, to acquire both. It may even have given him the moral green light to apply whatever means he could to get what he felt he was owed.

Many of us grow up with a relationship to God not dissimilar to Jacob's. If no one any longer believes that God is for the English, many who grow up in Christian homes may well sense that God is on their side. To the extent that this opens the door to further spiritual development, it is a blessing. But to the extent that it allows me to do as I please, with a vague feeling that God will not let me go, it is dangerous.

And if that is the extent of our belief, it is certainly not faith. It may, of course, give us the confidence to achieve the unthinkable, to take risks and to win against astounding odds, but it is not faith. Even after we make an initial commitment, talking to God in prayer, giving our lives over to him, asking for the forgiveness of our sins, it is easy to slip back into a relationship-as-magic view. If we are not very careful, we can see God as the way to get whatever we want. To me, the great danger of the 'healthy, wealth and wise' view of Christian success is that it

leads up this very cul-de-sac. It may look very spiritual. It may
be a long and very pleasant cul-de-sac. But it does not lead anywhere worthwhile. Whatever we say, it is hard to focus on the
One who blesses while paying so much attention to the blessings themselves.

And God is not going to leave Jacob there. God meets Jacob
on his lonely flight from his brother to his uncle. As we have
noted, God does not deliver a warning about Jacob's recent
behaviour nor about the way in which he is messing things up.
Surprisingly perhaps, God endorses the promises already made
and re-affirms his plan to bless Jacob (Gen 28:10-20).

Whether absolutely alone, or accompanied by a servant or
two, Jacob is profoundly moved by this encounter (Gen 28:16
and 17): 'When Jacob awoke from his sleep, he thought, "Surely
the LORD is in this place, and I was not aware of it." He was
afraid and said, "How awesome is this place! This is none other
than the house of God; this is the gate of heaven."'

This passage came to mean a lot to me as a postgraduate student. Don't ask me why, but I decided that my friends were having fun trips all over the world, and I wanted some fun. My
supervisor concurred, and I wrote to a number of US academic
and industrial specialists in my field of research. Many were in
California and so I wrote to a pastor I knew there, hoping to stay
at his place. He was very welcoming and, despite the fact that I
only checked the location of his place and the laboratories I
needed to visit after putting arrangements in place, everything
was within striking distance. At that moment when the wheels
of the plane finally left the tarmac, I remember thinking that
there was no going back – and I thought of Jacob setting out on
the adventure of his life to a new world. I remember realising
how it is when you set off into the unknown – with God. The
other person I thought about was Elisha, smashing the water
with his late mentor's cloak and asking if God would work for
him, too (2 Kings 2:11-14).

I was only away for a couple of weeks – but God showed he
was there, underpinning the relationships and seeing me
through. I had a great time, gained an exciting perspective on
my research field and met some very unusual people who made
time for me in their busy diaries.

One to one

To me, this experience marks two developments in the relationship. First, Jacob sees that there is a personal dimension to approaching God. Perhaps his attempt to do a deal there by that lonely stone was his first attempt to relate to God in the way he did with any other person.

But Jacob does not see God as any other person. The second big development is that Jacob gains a sense of awe. Jacob is scared of God. If we have any imagination at all, it is not hard to see why. Waking alone in the desert, perhaps the stars still bright in dark skies unpolluted by streetlights, a chill in the breeze with the sand still warm below the surface, I would feel emotionally raw, too. But the physical setting only provides the framework for this spiritual encounter. God is not out to frighten the day-lights out of Jacob. Perhaps that is why, if Jacob's surroundings and dream are so unnerving, the message itself is so reassuring and full of hope. While the experience itself does not change Jacob overnight, it is one he does not forget. Years later, with a crowd of descendants and dependants, Jacob makes his way back there to fulfil his side of the bargain he struck that night.

I have been following ITV's screening of the Alpha talks introduced by David Frost and have been interested in the young people's response during the discussion session to the proposition of having a personal relationship with God. As I understand their problem, they have no difficulty with a relationship, provided it is with someone they can see and interact with. Interestingly enough, the key relationship to emerge was that with their mothers. They felt they understood that relationship, and other relationships were, as I recall, discussed in terms of how they compared with that. But how can they have a relationship with... with whom? I am not a very good listener in these situations, and I was dying to explore relationships that they may have had with people whom they could not see or interact with in that way. Years ago we might have explored a courtship carried out by correspondence (sometimes writing letters to one another can be a very fruitful way of enriching a relationship, even today). However, the obvious modern analogy is with e-mail, where people really do get hooked on each other without ever meeting up. In fact, one of the great dangers of this type of relationship is that it is possible to hide so much – to be whoever you want to be – and still establish a relationship. But it happens. I was even reading in the paper the other day of a couple who put their DIY project on the Internet. Now the wife is leaving to live with someone who first met her there. These are quite negative examples, but it would have been fun to start with something like that and to see where the discussion went.

On the whole, I am not sure that the person-to-person relationship is the main stumbling block to our generation. Mobile 'phone adverts, and indeed the increasing reliance on all sorts of communication tools to establish a range of social and business relationships, I think, make it easier than ever to overcome the physical obstacles to having a personal relationship.

Perhaps the concept of God as a person is a much more severe test for our generation. With so much pantheism and mysticism about, people find it much easier to imagine God in terms of a force, an influence, a sort of sum of the good things in life or in the population. In fact, this story of Jacob, alone in the desert, conscious of the spiritual, the numinous, probably relates well to our generation. Perhaps something of his surprise would be our generation's surprise, too.

Awesome!

Undoubtedly, for Christians today, it is the sense of awe that is missing. When I read this story I am confronted, again, with my own lack of awe. I think people are looking for a sense of awe. I think people who enjoy the silence and solemnity of large churches are seeking it. I suspect Stanley Kubric was after it when he wove the Blue Danube into those wonderful space shots in his film, *2001, A Space Odyssey*. It is hard to watch Niagara Falls, or even, from the right perspective, a sunset without a sense of awe.

But to live our lives in the light of such awe, to be awed and happy, to be amazed and joyous, these are things we seldom attain, even in our spiritual lives. Of course one way to bring the two together is to thank and praise God every time we have an awesome experience – whether it be in connection with our work, our worship, our family life, or our leisure (not that these need be mutually exclusive).

In a sense the science fiction directors are onto a winner. The heavens were meant to awe, or perhaps it would be better to say we were meant to be awed by the heavens. The psalmists drew great comfort and strength from looking up:

> The heavens declare the glory of God;
> the skies proclaim the work of his hands.
>
> Day after day they pour forth speech;
> night after night they display knowledge.
>
> There is no speech or language
> where their voice is not heard.
>
> Their voice goes out into all the earth,
> their words to the ends of the world. (Psalm 19:1-4)

> When I consider your heavens,
> the work of your fingers,
>
> the moon and the stars,
> which you have set in place,
>
> what is man that you are mindful of him,
> the son of man that you care for him? (Psalm 8:3 and 4)

Looking up and around is a sound way into worship. The heavens are meant to lead us back to the Creator in our praise and worship. In each of the psalms above (and there are many others that resonate with the same theme), the poet takes time out to weave together a note of praise to God for the wonderful world around. And for me, some of my most moving spiritual experiences have come as I have tried to pull things together as a poem or even a song.

I realise that many of my memorable awesome experiences have not been in church. Looking out of the window of a plane and seeing a swirling hole in the sunset-drenched clouds was an example. Although it is only very recently that people have been able to suspend themselves in the clouds, it has not stopped God from painting scenery that is beautiful even from there. Watching a Vulcan take off, the whole world shaking through my feet and my tinnitus clanging like an alarm bell inside, was another of those experiences. Sometimes even the TV and radio can open up marvellous pathways to reverence. There was something on composites where they got talking about apples. I think I remember that apples are about 80 percent water, yet you can bite one open and the water doesn't run out. It may not even drip. That is a staggering piece of design.

Fortunately, we do have those moments in church too. Sometimes it is in singing a great hymn where the words and the music and our experience come together to reveal a sense of the majesty and power of God. Perhaps the worship in your church brings you right into the very presence of God and, again, you find yourself lost in 'wonder, love and praise.' But I am conscious of the need for more awe in my life, especially in my day-to-day life. You may find, having thought about this passage, that you are, too.

And once in a while, there will be that unexpected encounter – the one where God comes after you. Jacob did not set out to have the dream, but God set out to make contact with Jacob.

I am not preaching experiential highs. We have too many Christians who look for a quick charge on a Sunday but fail to enjoy a sense of awe in their lives as a whole. I am not sure that churches that 'do worship' well, will have fewer people in need of a sense of awe than those that leave people to find their own way through with quiet contemplation. However others may view us, we need a sense of awe in approaching God and we will not get far without it. Here we see how God met the requirement in Jacob's life.

And finally, an awareness of what is irreverent is not necessarily evidence of a proper sense of awe. Just because I can recognise that someone else is getting it wrong does not make me an expert. We may criticise the Government for the latest crisis, whatever it is, but we know inside we would do no better.

But irreverence provides a window on our problem here. In our world, irreverence is a virtue. Irreverent humour has broken free of the taboos and conventions that shackled our parents and has freed us to laugh at their foibles. We are told how important we are as individuals, how valid our perspectives are, how necessary it is that others should listen to us. We watch and read media streams only too willing to point out the failures of those whom we might traditionally have respected. In watching or working up sketches at church, I have seen how easy it is, in pursuing a creative and entertaining approach, to slip into irreverence. It all creates an environment where awe is difficult today.

Certainly, the generation coming up is subjected to a diet of education and entertainment so questioning, challenging, irreverent and self-focused, that awe of a God outside is a very difficult concept.

But it has always been difficult. Had it not been difficult for

Jacob, he could have acquired it at home. Why wait until he is established as a person if it could have been offered earlier? I suspect that God still offers the opportunity to learn awe today. Certainly Jacob cannot go much further until he has his first taste of it.

Quick-change artist?

So why doesn't Jacob change overnight? Quite literally overnight! Why isn't he like Paul whose life is transformed by a similar encounter while he, too, was on his way out of Canaan (e.g. Acts 22:6-11)?

I guess our understanding of what is happening in Jacob's life will be mediated to some extent by our New Testament view of conversion. I was brought up to believe that we all start our lives alienated from God but that through Jesus' sacrificial death, we can be reconciled to God. When I come to God in an encounter of conversion, asking for forgiveness and handing my life over to him, God promises to cancel my sin and take me on as his child. To seal this relationship, God the Holy Spirit comes and lives in me. There, he starts to bring my daily life into line with the legal position he has already conferred upon me, gifting and empowering me for whatever plans he has for my life. My side of this bargain is to be baptised as soon as I can. And that is still basically what I believe. This places a huge emphasis upon the conversion experience. Taking this view, the first, real encounter with God becomes vital, the touchstone of all subsequent experience.

I am conscious that many Christians will not see it quite this way. Some will believe that baptism as an infant confers special status and that coming formally into the church through, say, confirmation, completes the conversion/baptism experience described above. Others have quite detailed ideas about the sequence of events as far as conversion, water baptism and baptism by the Holy Spirit are concerned. I said 'basically' above because I have become aware over the years how many different approaches there are to conversion, and have met so many people who are clearly part of God's family (from their beliefs, behaviour and the fruit their lives bear) who will neither agree with, nor fit exactly into, the scheme I have outlined above.

Nor is my theology free from difficulty. What about the baptised believer who throws it all over and goes back to his or her old life? I remember arguing this through with the Roman Catholic chaplain at university one day. He felt that to throw doubt on the validity of the original conversion in the light of subsequent behaviour was a cop out. At the time I was more into arguing my case than listening to how he tried to fit the pieces together, so I cannot give you his particular approach. However, he has a point.

Increasingly we are seeing people who do not seem to have a single conversion event. They may always have been there, of course. I know, as a child, I asked Jesus to come into my heart more than once and was never quite sure that I was secure as a Christian. In fact, Christian assurance was something I struggled with for a long time. But the extended process where someone, for instance, shows an interest in Christianity and over a period of weeks, months, or even longer, moves to a position of faith is something that we seem to be seeing more of in our church, and I hear from others with the same experience.

I find John's Gospel helpful in this respect. I am very fortunate because I have the Bible on my laptop as I write, but I first did this exercise the hard way by working back and forth through the gospel. Let's take John on 'belief'. If you run the word, 'believe' through your search engine, you find that people are always coming to believe new things. Their state of belief keeps changing. Let's start with Nathaniel (John 1:43-51, a passage that alludes directly back to Jacob's dream that night). Nathaniel has lauded Jesus as the Son of God and the King of Israel. Jesus challenges or commends him – I am not quite sure which – over the quality of evidence he has for this announcement and promises him 'greater things'. Later on (John 2:11), we read that the disciples put their faith in Jesus after the wedding at Cana. After years of teaching on belief, we have Jesus exclaiming, 'You believe at last!' (John 16:31) to his disciples at their last meal together. Later still, one disciple, presumably John, enters the empty tomb (John 20:8). We read that he 'saw and believed.' You can fill in the gaps, but my question is, what did they believe at each of these steps? Certainly, they believed something new, grasped some new truth each time. However, it is not clear to me that Nathaniel, for instance, at that first encounter with Jesus had a real grasp of what saving faith was all about. I am not suggesting that conversion is an endless process in which we converge, ultimately, on salvation. Far from it – there are plenty of examples in the New Testament of people whose lives were changed instantly, and plenty of examples today that leave me convinced that instant and effective conversion is possible and even desirable. All I am saying is that there is some warrant from scripture for an understanding that even an encounter may lead to a conversion experience that is part of a process rather than a point event.

But this may not completely alleviate our difficulties over the fact that Jacob does not seem to change very much, despite this intense experience. Surely he would have relied more on God and less on his own schemes.

As we look ahead, the funny side of Jacob's life with his uncle is the way they are each out to get the most from the other. Thrown together by family and fate, they set out to exploit each other to the full, Laban going for low-cost labour, Jacob setting out to grow a huge herd from the meagre potential of Laban's leftovers. There is a flavour of this in the film, Maverick, where the leading couple (played by Mel Gibson and Jodie Foster) are drawn together by chemistry and a love of poker. Because they are both cheats, she spends quite a bit of the plot trying to steal from him, and he smiles and tries to recover it, while they temporarily collaborate against the outside world. And thus it is with Jacob and Laban – a delicate dance choreographed by necessity with each man's hand never far from the other's pocket.

Jacob does not seem to have changed, he has only become more so.

And it happens, doesn't it? Someone becomes a Christian, but he still won't go out and get a job. She says she has found the Lord, but she is still a terrible flirt. Sometimes the problem is simply a lack of teaching or an unwillingness to let God work. At other times though, it seems to show how deeply ingrained some behaviour is, how innately it defines us, how, in a sense, we will never shake it off. Sometimes the characteristic needs to be redeemed because it will never be removed.

Watching Jacob is a good way of seeing how this can happen. Jacob will always enjoy a good bargain. Jacob will always be competitive. I remember George Verwer of Operation Mobilization, telling how he watches the lights in the other direction when waiting at a red light, so that he can get away at the first opportunity. George Verwer will always be competitive and impatient. And over the years, God has channelled that competitive energy and eagerness into his service.

What next?

The narrative moves on to Jacob's time with his uncle and his growing family. Because his family life is so complex and because we have very complex family arrangements today, and also because the whole concept of fatherhood is up for debate, we will try to look at this as a block of material in chapter 6.

However, there are some things that happen to Jacob over the next twenty or more years that relate to his spiritual growth.

A big thing, of course, is that Jacob matures as a man. He sweats and slogs and sees his own children grow up to join him in the fields. That certainly gives a man a different perspective. I was chatting to a school friend recently, and he was saying how much less stressed life was after 40. From the chuckle I guess he meant that the pressures were greater, but somehow it didn't matter quite as much.

I tend to take things quite simply, and so I assume Jacob was over forty (taking a hint from Gen 26:34) when he left home, and must have been in his sixties, at least, when he returned from serving fourteen years in total for Leah and Rachel, and six years for the herd (Gen 31:41). That still left plenty of time to grow old gracefully before meeting Pharaoh at 130 or dying at 147. It seems an incredible age to us, although our grandchildren may approach the figures with a more open-minded view of old age. I do not understand the business of aging well enough to comment further, but I appreciate that these numbers present a difficulty.

However you handle the business of Jacob's age, from a fractional point of view the time with Laban represents a fairly modest slice of his life coming up to middle age. If we divide all the numbers by two, we get some sort of feel for how the events might stack up in our lives, mid-twenties to mid-thirties, perhaps. And during this period, God begins to talk to Jacob. Again, it is hard to know exactly, but by the end of this era, Jacob is not surprised when God talks to him. We may guess that the relationship has been developing during those years. God speaks to him in Genesis 31:3 when he tells Jacob it is time to move on. Then there is his dream about the flocks (Gen 31:10-13), at which God also tells him once more that it is time to return home.

As we go along, I hope you can see Jacob accumulating the relevant elements of a meaningful relationship with God. From a start that might be hard to differentiate from superstition, he has moved to understand that the God who enjoyed a personal relationship with his father and grandfather is personally interested in him, too. He has a sense of awe and is beginning to fear this God. And now the communication channels are opening up.

How about you? Do you have any meaningful communication with God these days? Whoa! I have friends, you say, who are always telling me how God has directed them to do this or that and, quite frankly, their lives just go round in circles. They always have very clear ideas about what God is saying about my life, too. Perhaps you would go further and say that you are not interested in a relationship like that. Perhaps you feel uneasy about their superspirituality or the intensity that comes across whenever you meet them.

It is a tricky problem and one that I suspect Jesus was aware of when he told us to watch for fruit (e.g. Matt 7:16-20), rather than listening to what people say about themselves. I remember once going around the final year students' projects, trying to get a feel for what lay in store for me. One project looked very interesting. The chap who had done the work was standing by, and gave what I can only describe as a very impressive spiel. I felt sure this chap was at the top of the class. I was surprised a few weeks later to see his name well down on the list. I even tried to badger a tutor whom we had in common to tell me why there had been such a serious miscarriage of academic justice. My tutor was very professional and refused to give anything away, but I reached the conclusion that perhaps the student had not performed as original or thorough a piece of work as he believed. Despite the experience, I often find myself taking people at their own evaluation – and it can even happen in church.

The key here is the fruit. If you find someone who talks up their relationship with God but who always has a gripe, who can always tell you where other Christians are failing, whose life seems never to get anywhere, you may have cause to be cautious. R T Kendall in his book, *Just Grace*, notes the temptation to create an aura of holiness by telling everyone what God has said to us. Phrases such as, 'God has told me to...' can stimulate undue deference in other Christians. There is a danger that this type of talk amounts to little more than performing our alms-giving in public or making a song and dance about our fasting.

But where you find the fruit, you should listen. The cheerful, godly Christian has something to say, whether or not he or she sprinkles the conversation with references to what God is doing.

Again, I do not want to be misunderstood. It is not the talk that matters, it is the fruit. No fruit with or without the talk is useless. Fruit with or without the talk is vital.

So, has God started to speak to you yet? Jacob is refreshingly real as a person, and yet God starts to speak to him. He is a shep-herd, a hands-on man, and yet God speaks to him. When it is time to move on, God tells him. I think guidance is often diffi-cult in the immediate decision, but it is possible to know how far you are from your Heavenly Father. It is possible to have a sense of peace that you are in the right place, or to have a growing dis-quiet and sense that God is moving you on. It is possible to be surprised by the way your daily reading stacks up in triplicate, bringing the same piece of advice home time and again. It is possible to hear God's voice through godly friends and in other ways, some of which can be quite spectacular. It is possible to realise that the relationship is becoming strained or distant. Jacob has some spectacular experiences, and although he is also a man's man, he learns to hear the voice of God.

Distant relations

Yet even at this point, there still seems to be some distance in the relationship. I may well be reading this wrongly, but when he swears the treaty with Laban as they finally part in peace, he does so in the name of the 'Fear of his father Isaac' (Gen 31:53). Why does he not acknowledge God as his God? Perhaps it is the custom of the day not to sound too presumptuous. However, he knows that Laban has already encountered God, and, indeed, it is only this divine intervention that has enabled Jacob to save face and depart in peace. Maybe there is something in the cul-tural backdrop that we can no longer appreciate.

But maybe Jacob is a little ashamed. Maybe he has some insight into his predicament and is a little embarrassed that this powerful, upright God has had to defend Jacob whose behaviour has not been blameless. I am not a great person for putting stickers in my car. I disliked the 'Baby on Board' diamonds when we had babies, and never really worked out what they were saying. I am sure there will be readers who found them very useful, but they seemed too much of an accessory for me. As a disabled driver, I have never wanted a sticker in my window proclaiming the fact (although I am quite happy to have the badge and the clock on my dashboard for free parking). Apart from my natural disinclination towards badges, however, I have another reason for not putting a fish on my car. I am not sure my behaviour would always show off the fish to best effect. You perform some original manoeuvre in traffic, and the last thing the green car that had to brake heavily sees of you is a fish, as you head for cover. I remember refusing to slow down, and swerving past a lady who was backing off her drive, grimacing as I went past. I was certainly in the right, but Dani pulled me up over it, complaining that she knew the lady from queuing up at the school in the mornings.

People at work are quick to point out the Christian with the fish who is a bit of a dodgy customer, a pain to work with, or who cuts too many corners. Many of us settle for something a little more distant. Let's not drag God into this. Anything for a quiet life. Now and then, we get flushed out of the undergrowth – someone will round on us and say, 'You're a Christian! What do you think about this?' And then it can get a little embarrassing. I just wonder if that is how Jacob felt.

Incidentally, I am not for or against wearing a fish. I believe that people should be convinced you are a Christian from what they see of your life. If wearing a badge or whatever helps, that is terrific.

My guess is that there are lots of us at this same stage in the development of our faith. We have a knowledge of God, some experience of being guided and led, but the relationship is still a little distant.

Wrestling with God

There is another unexpected blast of blessing, when the angels meet up with Jacob at Mahanaim (Gen 32:1). Isn't this just what we would expect of God – to remind Jacob of his promises to him and to provide an enriching experience once more?

But the big encounter here is the midnight wrestling match.

As we would expect of Jacob, he has prepared as thoroughly as he can for his reunion with Esau. The size of Esau's escort (Gen 32:6) convinces him that there is trouble ahead. Having escaped the frying pan of Laban's anger, is he to fall into the fire of Esau's wrath? He puts every grain of skill into preparing the way, from the first scouts he sent ahead with their message of appeasement (Gen 32:3-5). Dividing the party in two (Gen 32: 7) is a smart move, and then we find Jacob praying. After that he adopts more skilful tactics, as he sends wave after wave of gifts ahead of him (Gen 32:13-21), coaching each drover carefully to get his lines just right. Finally, he puts his family and all his possessions between himself and Esau on the other side of the river and spends the night alone. It is probably the first time he has been alone for many, many years. Perhaps it is his first night alone since that dramatic journey to his uncle Laban.

Catastrophic circumstances always bring out the best and the worst in us. Cautious Jacob is naturally pessimistic about the future here and can only imagine an enraged Esau catching up with him after two decades. He has sufficient imagination to envisage the various possibilities, and his natural instincts are to prepare for the worst. Why doesn't he pray about it? Well he has prayed! Why doesn't he leave it there?

A personal perspective

I'm alone just now as I tap away on my laptop. I have that agonising choice ahead that will affect the family. I have now left my last job on a package about six weeks ago and the two options I had at the time have continued to develop – but not at the same speed. One is ready and they want an answer in a couple of days. One will take a few more weeks to mature. One lets me work locally, the other means new schools for the children, a house move and finding a new church. The job that is not yet quite ready has a lot of attraction for me personally. It is the Chair.

Dani and I have prayed about the decision. But what after you have prayed? Jesus warns us about repeating the same thing endlessly and reminds us that God is well aware of our needs (Matt 6:7 and 8): 'And when you pray, do not keep on babbling like pagans, for they think they will be heard because of their many words. Do not be like them, for your Father knows what you need before you ask him.' It is at times like this that Jacob comes alive as a character.

In fact, this whole study of Jacob, making real decisions in a hostile world, has come at a great time for me. Now it is the day of the decision. I have spoken to so many people whom I respect, Christians and secular people. We have examined it from every angle. We have prayed and fasted and, after waking a little early, today is the day when I must accept or decline one offer, before the other is fully mature. We are going for the academic job that has yet to mature, although it will mean a family move. From a personal point of view, two things have been very helpful in hearing God's voice. Dani's daily psalm, in her through-the-year Bible, is from the start of Psalm 107(1-7):

Give thanks to the LORD, for he is good;
his love endures forever.

Let the redeemed of the LORD say this -
those he redeemed from the hand of the foe,

those he gathered from the lands,
from east and west, from north and south.

Some wandered in desert wastelands,
finding no way to a city where they could settle.

They were hungry and thirsty,
and their lives ebbed away.

Then they cried out to the LORD in their trouble,
and he delivered them from their distress.

He led them by a straight way
to a city where they could settle.

It provides a wonderful reminder of God's ability to see us through, even where we cannot see. The bit about God finding us a home is reassuring too, although the main encouragement is that, should we strike out in the wrong direction, God is able to bring us back. This is not the whole story; other things are falling into place. Dani approached a number of schools in the area, and only one, in a village we would be interested in, has responded. Today's reading on our daily calendar was also surprisingly encouraging. The brief meditation, from Charles Swindoll's Stress Fractures says: 'Contrary to popular opinion, anyone who sincerely seeks God's will can find it.' The accompanying verse is, 'Ask and it will be given to you; seek and you will find; knock and the door will be opened to you' (Matt 7:7).

I know there is a danger of using the Bible as a hit and miss source of guidance. We can even use daily readings as a sort of Christian version of a horoscope, seeking arcane references to our situation. But over this period, God has been doing for us what he did for Jacob – reassuring us that we are loved and that he is able to look after us. I don't know whether we are going to get this right, but I know that God will bring us to the right place in the end.

Thinking it through

1. How many ways do we act that show we still treat our faith as if it were magic rather than about relationships?

2. What was your most recent life-changing encounter with God? What will you take into your life from it?

3. If you look at the different lessons Jacob learned in his relationship with God, how many have you already learned? What do you think might be next on the list?

4. When did you last have a sense of awe? How did you respond?

5. List three events during the past six months through which God has shown that he cares about you personally.

6. A friend is moving house with her job. Should she start looking for a house near a church, near work, or in a good school catchment area? How do you think she should go about the task?

7. In a surprise move, your pastor tells you he is off for a place on the board of a rapidly expanding information company. What goes through your mind?

8. With whom do you struggle most at work? Are they like you in any way? What is God teaching you through the encounter?

9. List the key events in your life to date. Put down one thing God has taught you through each event. Now what do you make of the pattern?

10. Is there anything you have been after for the past few years that you are now not so sure was worth the effort? What will you do now?

4

Coming Home

And then, whack! Someone is on top of him. Smack! Thump!
Pound! Someone is beating the living daylights out of him.
Swivelling and turning in the darkness, Jacob has no idea of
what is happening. Twist! Wrench! What is going on here? Kick!
Maybe that will give him something to think about! Aaarrrgggh!
How did he get round there? Slowly Jacob moves the fight from
sheer survival to a more even competition. Jacob has been up all
night before, protecting and looking after the flock. Jacob's mus-
cles have been toned by two decades of hard labour. Jacob's
days among the tents are a distant memory and he has developed a whole new layer of rugged armour to add to his formidable skills.

Crunch! As the jarring and parrying continues, Jacob has time
to think. He realises that this is not a bandit. Bandits slit your
throat and make off with your possessions. This man is not in
the throat-slitting business and anyway, any sane bandit, having
spied out this wealthy party would be plundering away on the
other side of the river. Any sane bandit might well be keeping a
healthy eye on Esau's progress, too.

Perhaps Jacob starts checking off a list of possible motives this
chap might have. If you know the motive, you can start to bargain. But there is no clear motive. Can he beat the chap and have
done with it? Will he need to buy him off? What sort of tactics
spin through your mind as you struggle for a foothold in the
dark? Maybe it looks like, having failed to cash in on his surprise attack, Jacob's assailant may go under as Jacob flexes every
muscle in search of victory. But while the result may sway in the
balance, it falls to neither. For hours they sweat and grunt, taking the punishment, dishing it out.

The longest hymn in our hymnbook is by Charles Wesley
('Come, O Thou traveller unknown') and it is about this very
fight. However, even if we were to sing all the verses, we would
get no concept of the length of this gruelling duel.

Somehow, some time that night Jacob realises that God is

behind all this. The text is not clear, but the most obvious reading is that somehow God comes down to wrestle with Jacob. It is not a natural inference that this dreadful attack, coming when Jacob was at his lowest ebb, torn between fear and uncertainty, is actually the hand of God. If Jacob's world is full of foes, if his only meaningful relationships have been adversarial, God will tackle him as an opponent. And in the struggle Jacob forges a new relationship.

I wonder how long it takes us to see the hand of God in that diagnosis three weeks ago and the treatment we are just about to endure. I wonder whether we see the hand of a loving Father behind that bruising viva we have just failed. Jacob's great discovery here, as far as I can see, lies in recognising the scope for blessing. If his innate pessimism has left him isolated, afraid and alone by the riverbank, some piece of blinding faith has enabled him to grasp this as an opportunity for blessing. The blessing!

Jacob pours every drop of determination and vigour into a renewed attempt to wrestle his opponent to the ground. And his opponent takes a short-cut to victory by throwing Jacob's hip out of joint. The text indicates that he had only to touch it. And still Jacob does not give up. Despite the searing pain of dislocation, Jacob hangs in there – switching back to survival mode once more. This combatant may win, but he will not get away.

Perhaps it was not until daybreak that they spoke at all. Certainly the conversation comes alive then and Jacob enters in on the bargain of his life. So what is going on here? Well, it is not easy to say. Something spectacular is happening when God feels he must bless someone in this way. Other times when a blessing is wrenched out like this occur when Jesus comes across a piece of stupendous faith – the woman with the haemorrhage (e.g. Mark 5:25-34) or the woman from Syrian Phoenicia (Mark 7:24-30) – and it is probably not a bad guess to suspect that there is a large slice of faith in Jacob's reaction here.

It seems to me that the big leap of faith that Jacob has made lies in identifying this blessing with a person. It is through this man that he will be blessed. His blessing is not a piece of magic that hangs around his family and generally makes life more pleasant for the lucky son. Nor is it a blessing given by an all-powerful God who takes little interest in the bestowal. Jacob has engaged with God. From now on, he will see the blessing in terms of a relationship. And that is what God intends for each of us.

Broken bones

So, if God intends to bless Jacob, why maim him and inflict a legacy of impairment and pain on him? Is there a cathartic motive here, enabling Jacob to come to terms with his past, perhaps even to atone for it? Some may read it that way, but I would struggle to do so.

In terms of the flow of the narrative, Jacob's dislocated hip marks a break in the journey. He had run, fled, walked and meandered up to this point. He will limp to the end of his days. I hope you have the text near you and catch the cadences (Gen 32:31): 'The sun rose above him as he passed Peniel, and he was limping because of his hip.' Simple, elegant phrasing, but things have changed.

So what has changed? Well, his name has been changed, for a start. No longer Jacob, the deceiver, but Israel, who strives with God and prevails. So what else has changed? Well, Jacob has one strength fewer to play to. I believe God wants Jacob to come to the end of his strength. Although we have noted the way in which God has been determined to bless Jacob and has protected him, at times in ways that Jacob has only discovered later, much of Jacob's success is characterised by his own efforts. The wealth around him is due to his exertions, the edgy relationships a product of his sharp practice.

From now on, it will be different. Jacob will not be able to work his socks off, because one sock will dangle on a dodgy leg. Nor will he be able to run the next time a relationship goes sour. Jacob will have to rely more heavily on the God he wrestled with for his material blessings and for daily protection. From now on, life will go a little more slowly. But it is going to be OK.

Our attitude to disability is mixed. There are those who believe God wants all his children to enjoy the best of health. A failure to be healed is evidence of a lack of faith, a clear departure from God's best plan for one's life. Most Christians do not subscribe to the more extreme form of this doctrine. We know that the blind man in John 9 was not blind because of his sin, or that of anyone else. There are all sorts of books where people relate the way in which a serious illness or injury has been used by God to build up the individual and bring blessing to those around them. Joni Eareckson-Tada's output is perhaps among the best known, but there is plenty more material on the market. We can see that God can bring good out of disaster. But Jacob seems to tell us something even more alarming. It seems that God is responsible for the disaster as well.

And sometimes God is willing to draw in the circle of our capabilities, to limit our potential, to close down opportunities in order that our walk with him might be closer and more reliant on him. Sometimes God shuts us down to give us time. I remember listening to Brash Bonsall, the founder of the Birmingham Bible Institute, as an old man explaining how a serious spell of illness had put him flat on his back. He said that when you were flat on your back, it was a good time to look up and he went on to explain how he had had the vision for a Christian training facility during that illness.

As a more recent example, I had been circulating a manuscript for publication for a while. It was my first attempt to write a whole book and (as everyone tells you it will be) there were no openings. In a renewed effort, I opened up a new line of enquiry that resulted in an invitation to submit the manuscript. The day after it went in, the editor phoned to say that he had injured himself gardening and, being unable to garden, had picked up the manuscript. Sad as I was for his pain, for me it meant he had the time to look at something he might otherwise have left for a little longer. But what if there is no clear pay-off?

I read on a wall at university that old professors never die, they just lose their faculties. And losing our faculties is, perhaps, a wider issue. We live in a world afraid of growing old, encouraging us to insure against every eventuality. Does Jacob's experience of disability help us to deal with the midlife heart attack, the back problem that becomes debilitating, the diagnosis of diabetes or whatever? I think there is something in this, but it is not easy.

A friend of mine was badly injured in a road accident on an aid trip to Romania. Somehow he was scalded by water from the radiator. Following this he discovered he had leukaemia. Overall, he found himself with quite a lot of free time at his disposal. I remember asking him whether he was getting lots of good meditation in. His honest answer was that he was finding it hard to put in time with his Bible. God has been reaping fruit from his life, but it has not been a magical, overnight experience. Simply creating time in our lives does not make us holy. In fact the temptation to watch a bit more sport, a few more soaps, read the paper a bit more thoroughly, or pick up extra magazines may ultimately have the opposite effect. However, more time can give us a chance to evaluate our lifestyle and the way we are living. Dani and I have sometimes found that a holiday helps to do that, too.

Does God have anything else in mind when he makes us limp where others run? I may have an edge over you here, because I have never run in my life. I guess I must have stunned my parents when I arrived. They were missionaries, serving God in the Middle East. Maybe God would work a miracle! At times I have sat alone in a hotel room in the US, Germany, or (once) Japan and realised that God has been working – but not like that. I know God spoke to my Dad through Jesus' words to Peter during the feet-washing episode: 'You do not realize now what I am doing, but later you will understand' (John 13:7). I also remember seeing Psalm 147:10 underlined in my Mom's Schofield Bible. In the NIV, it reads:

His pleasure is not in the strength of the horse,
    nor his delight in the legs of a man;

I think if we can get it right (and it may take years to do so), the ultimate benefit of restricted options is an increased dependence on God. I say, 'if', because one can be too willing to be dependent, too willing to let others take the burden. There is an extent to which you need a fierce sense of independence to keep an illness or disability from dominating your life. The mix of spiritual dependence with physical independence is a really tricky recipe and balance is not easy.

A friend at church has had Parkinson's disease for a number of years and is entirely incapacitated. I remember writing to him at the time he had to surrender his driving licence because I could see both the need to give way to the inevitable and the need to keep pressing for as much freedom as possible in an ever constricting world. Inside there was the need in the end for him to give in gracefully without becoming gritty, frustrated, and ultimately an unpleasant person. I could see the humiliation in losing his licence and the determination that had enabled him to keep it that far. I felt helpless for him but wrote a short note all the same.

And I have learned to push back the boundaries. I hated wearing artificial legs in the humidity and heat of Dubai where my parents spent almost a decade. They made me put them on for a while every day and it was always a great relief when I could persuade either parent that it was time to take them off. And yet something of that early discipline and perhaps some inherited stubbornness that comes from the sort of people who will leave good prospects at home and immerse themselves in another world, has made me a very determined person. People tell me how relentlessly unyielding they find me and I think it has taken Dani, a nice middle-class girl, years to get used to this focused and formidable husband she has married. Colleagues at work talk of my work rate and energy and ask Dani if I am as focused and busy at home.

All this comes with penalties: an iron will struggles to become dependent. It struggles in other areas, too. In assessing the progress others make, it underestimates the difficulties they face. It can be very impatient. It can tune out the negative messages, since the negative messages have largely been wrong in the past. There is no such word as can't – until you are over 25 and working with people whose horizons appear to be constrained in many directions. For them there is can't and you must learn not to dismiss it as cant.

At the same time I have to depend for some things. Like top buttons on shirts and clip-on ties. And out of this incongruous combination, God is blending a character with strength and durability that learns to look to him. As I say, I can see a lot of myself in Jacob as he grits his teeth, in possession of yet another blessing, and starts the torturous journey to meet Esau.

The message before we move on with him is probably to take another look at that latest difficulty we encountered, that life-changing problem looming up ahead. The hand of God may be behind it. He may purpose to undermine some of our self-assurance in order that we may depend upon him.

Back to Bethel

And now Jacob leads his family back to Bethel (Gen 35:1-14), the place he has told them of many times, and there he leads the household in worship at a home-made altar. He does not try to strike a deal to cover the rest of his life. He simply worships.

The flow of the story is hard to piece together, but the intervening piece of news about the death of Rebekah's nurse, seems to indicate that Jacob stays at Bethel for a while.

How does God react to this? God does what he has been doing all along. He promises to bless Jacob. After endorsing the name change (Gen 35:10), God re-affirms the promises given to

Abraham and Isaac of a multitude of descendants and the land. Studying these passages again has reminded me just how much God cares for us. And here is the security that goes with the blessing – that God has a burning desire to bless his children, a purpose that does not diminish with the decades. And I guess that is all the security we need.

Sitting on my career decision, I have to say how refreshing and reassuring this is.

Jacob is not home yet. This watershed, when he leads his family in worship, does not erase his past. But Jacob has returned and put worship back at the centre of his life.

On to the end

Large tracts of time break up the story from here on. But Jacob at the end of his days has clearly been growing in faith (Gen 48:21): 'I am about to die, but God will be with you and take you back to the land of your fathers.' Jacob's prophecies in Genesis 49 are surefooted and insightful. Gone is the insecure Jacob who must negotiate and grab the best he can from every situation. Gone, too, the Jacob for whom life is sometimes a bit too much. He may have been pushed around in the past but, as we shall see when looking at his family relationships, he is not intimidated or outfoxed by the generation coming through.

Here is someone who understands what God is about, who sees that there is a grand canvas and who catches something of the sketch that has still not been painted in.

Here is someone who is secure. He fears nothing. He has stood before Pharaoh, the greatest human power in his world. He has argued the toss with Joseph, powerful and strong willed himself. He does not seem afraid of dying and the magnificent way in which he gathers his family around for that last conference, and then gathers his feet into the bed to die is both moving and profound.

Here is someone who has succeeded. His currency of flocks and herds is despised in Egypt, but what does he care. It may be a long stopover, but they are bound for somewhere where sheep and goats will once again provide the fabric of subsistence.

I think it would have been fun to have interviewed the aged Jacob, to have brought to him my dilemmas and decisions in life. I suspect that things look very simple from that end of life, and

he would probably have told me that it was actually very difficult to go wrong in the end, but that you can save yourself a lot
of aggro by getting the right focus from the start. My guess is he
would have told me: just learn to worship and do what you like.

Thinking it through

1. Have you ever wrestled with God? How long did it take?
   What did you learn?
2. This is the third night you have lain awake worrying about
   it. What are you going to do about it?
3. A gifted local speaker has just had a stroke. You hear that
   his speech is still badly slurred, and want to write. What
   would you say?
4. Think about two disabled people you know. To what extent
   has their disability had a positive impact on the character
   of each? If there has been a downside, what would you say
   it was?
5. A friend tells you her mother has had a bad fall and will be
   unable to live alone again. What options might you discuss
   with her?
6. You have a heart attack at fifty. What might God say to you
   through it?
7. What act of worship would you plan to celebrate your
   retirement?
8. How can we improve the quality of worship at dedications,
   marriages and funerals?
9. List three promises God has made to you and fulfilled so
   far in your life.
10. What sort of pension arrangements should a Christian
    make?
11. Are there three things you have learned through your
    worship in the past year that you have been able to put
    into practice? If not, how might you change your worship?
12. Your church has two people who share the task of leading
    worship. One you like and the other you struggle with.
    How can you improve the worship you offer on the weeks
    when your favourite is not on the platform?

5

A Question of Relationships

John writes (1 John 4:20): 'For anyone who does not love his brother, whom he has seen, cannot love God, whom he has not seen.' It is a bit of a tough one. Surely I can love God who is perfect, while loathing my unpleasant brother. Well, not according to John.

I hope you are now convinced that God wants to sort out Jacob's heavenward relationship before he can really bless him. But God uses other relationships to try and help this along. In fact, because Jacob's relationship with God is so difficult at the start, his other relationships also suffer. Jacob is not too hot on long-lasting relationships, at least not to start with. So let's start by looking at the lessons on relationships that Jacob learns from his relationships with others. In this chapter, we will focus on Jacob's interactions with Esau and Laban, and go on to look at Jacob as a father in the next chapter. Jacob's family is such a chaotic and interesting collection of colourful characters and explosive incidents that there will be more than enough for a single chapter.

In one sense, Jacob has a dream start to life. He is born into a family enjoying special blessings and even before he is born, there is a special prophecy about him. What can possibly go wrong?

Brothers!

I have three brothers and two sisters. I get the impression that we are much closer as a family than most – although as I write, we are spread out over three continents and four countries. Certainly, in-laws coming into family gatherings encounter a new sort of world. I am the eldest and, to that extent, I find it easier to identify with Esau than Jacob, at least in terms of taking the run of the world for granted.

I am not a twin, but there is a gap of only 14 months between me and the next brother in the family. And like Esau and Jacob, we have taken quite different routes. He is the outdoorsman, a carpenter in New England, who has built his own house in the woods. He drives a pick-up and creates beautiful houses that stand on the rocky shore and look out over the crashing Atlantic. I live in a brick house pretty much like all the other houses in our street.

Anyway, although we have always been very different, and had our tensions, we only once fought physically, as far as I can remember, and I came off very poorly. It was a bit of a shock to my pride (although I guess any one else would have predicted the result). I hadn't really analysed the incident until last year, when he mentioned it. I realised then how much he resented the fact that I was always left in charge when our parents were out.

And Jacob grows up under that sort of shadow. Esau will always be in charge. Esau will always have the run of the place. And the bulk of Isaac's wealth will come to Esau. We never had that problem because, since Dad and Mom were missionaries, there was never going to be much wealth to distribute – which I think makes for much better relationships anyway. Can Jacob change himself and escape the situation?

Family relationships are always the hardest in which to change yourself. Patterns become ingrained and they are hard to leave behind – even the trivial things. Because I was on crutches, my Dad always went up stairs behind me and came down them in front. He would still do it when I was a man. Your family remembers the 'real' you. Even when you want to change, you can so easily be sucked back into the old patterns, the old rules of precedence, the old ways of relating. And, of course, as the eldest, I am all in favour of the old ways!

And both brothers, in their own way, are highly competitive. Jacob is ambitious, conniving, scheming, determined. Esau, the successful hunter, the desirable son-in-law, must have been a tough and determined opponent. Jacob, with no visible means of rising above the situation, plays out his competition within it. The relationship seems to have nothing for Jacob and it looks as if Jacob has given up all hope of achieving anything from it. Perhaps he feels that trying to get on with Esau will be a one-way street, with Esau taking yet more of what he frankly feels is his. Maybe he thinks it would be interpreted as a further sign of weakness and he fears being despised. Maybe he doesn't think much about it and focuses on getting what he wants.

Scripture is quite clear that Esau was culpable in trading the birthright for a bowl of soup (Gen 25:27-34; Heb 12:16 and 17). But Jacob's ruthlessness in driving such a hard bargain must have further undermined the relationship. While we recognise that Esau will put his own spin on events, we are not entirely surprised to hear him complaining bitterly that he has been cheated twice (Gen 27:36) when Jacob finally succeeds in his second goal of taking the blessing, too.

So where does that take the relationship? Well, the relationship is dead in the water and there is nothing left for Jacob to do, but run (Gen 27:41-28:5).

Before we leave this, let us note that Isaac must take a large slice of responsibility for the friction between his sons, since he knew which way the blessing should go yet planned to give it the other way. In fact, in the story of the blessing, Isaac comes across as a weak father, driven by his own senses and desires, rather than what he knows God wants. Read the passage (Gen 27:1-41). It is all about Isaac's senses and the way they play for him and against him. His eyes that are failing prevent him from recognising the impostor. He wants another one of those tasty meals. His taste buds tell him that he has the right son. His ears warn him that something is wrong, but his nose and sense of touch reassure him that his plan is working. Nowhere do we find him seeking God's guidance in prayer. And no wonder! He knows that God has promised the blessing to someone else (Gen 25:23)

Uncles!

This pattern is repeated in Jacob's life when he meets Uncle Laban. A fresh start, a new relationship, no baggage. Surely here is a much more promising relationship, too, since the ground rules may allow Jacob a bit more room, and also they are more manifestly fair. The unfairness of suffering the discrimination as the younger twin is no longer an issue. Laban is an established farmer, with nothing to prove to, or to fear from, his young nephew. At least that is how it starts out. So how does the relationship develop? Is this a whole new ball game? Well, no – it ends in exactly the same way, with Jacob taking off suddenly, and leaving an irate relative behind.

The bust-up when Laban finally catches up with Jacob is

especially illuminating (Gen 31:22-54). Just listen to the tone of the argument.

Laban: 'What have you done? You've deceived me, and you've carried off my daughters like captives in war. Why did you run off secretly and deceive me? Why didn't you tell me, so I could send you away with joy and singing to the music of tambourines and harps? You didn't even let me kiss my grandchildren and my daughters good-bye. You have done a foolish thing.' (Gen 31:26b-28)

Jacob: 'What is my crime? What sin have I committed that you hunt me down? Now that you have searched through all my goods, what have you found that belongs to your household? Put it here in front of your relatives and mine, and let them judge between the two of us.

'I have been with you for twenty years now. Your sheep and goats have not miscarried, nor have I eaten rams from your flocks. I did not bring you animals torn by wild beasts; I bore the loss myself. And you demanded payment from me for whatever was stolen by day or night. This was my situation: The heat consumed me in the daytime and the cold at night, and sleep fled from my eyes. It was like this for the twenty years I was in your household. I worked for you fourteen years for your two daughters and six years for your flocks, and you changed my wages ten times.' (Gen 31:36-41)

Can you hear it? Neither side will admit to any wrongdoing. Who is right? Well, Genesis is quite clear that Laban has a point and that Jacob did deceive him in running off by stealth. Also, Laban is right in claiming that his household gods have been stolen, although Jacob is not wrong to repudiate the accusation because he does not realise that Rachel has stolen them (Gen 31:19,20,35). But no one doubts that Jacob's claims to having been wronged are valid, too.

Tangled relationships

Twice we have seen Jacob given a good start and twice it has turned sour. Twice it ends in serious conflict and twice Jacob takes off. We are not going to be able to pick all the goodness from this little tangle and it is certainly the sort of situation that will reward personal meditation. As I look into this, I see myself, my failures, and I see God's ability to steer me around. You will see different things. In a sense, these Old Testament biographies are wonderful mirrors in which we see what we are really like because the narrative reveals so thoroughly what these people were like. The trick is to remember what we see in the mirror (Jas 1:23-25).

Let's start with the parting recriminations. Clearly each one is only interested in his own case. Jacob cannot say, 'I'm sorry for deceiving you, and sneaking off while you were away shearing the sheep.' If he recognises his wrongdoing at all, he feels it is completely overshadowed by Laban's atrocious treatment for the past twenty years. Similarly, Laban, who took his nephew in when he was destitute, whose family and flocks have provided for all his emotional and material needs, cannot get over Jacob's abominable behaviour.

There is something here about what is currently called 'listening'. I have been told quite a lot in the past that I do not listen, and so I am an expert in not listening. And this is classical not listening behaviour. We remember all the times we have been wronged, all the times the opposition trumped our carefully selected hand, all the times we were put down, struggled unrewarded, or gave that bit extra – and then we bring it all up at the end, conveniently forgetting, or blissfully unaware of, the way in which our own efforts have undermined the situation.

A few years ago, I went on a management course that made a big impact on me. It has helped me to look back over some of the things I have done that perhaps created some of the negative reactions I encountered. Surprising reactions are not always quite so surprising when you look back. I remember winning a prize quite early on at work. It was worth a lot of money in my economy and I was the sole author of the paper for which it was awarded. Others had been involved in the research (and were meticulously acknowledged in the paper) and the company's publication rules meant that various bosses had had a hand in the amendments as the paper went through the approval process. If it happened again, I think I would have taken them all out for a drink, just to say thanks – even though I am still teetotal. I do not believe anyone felt it was unjust, but I guess that pocketing all that money without a nod in their direction must have been rough. Not that I was flush and could spare the cash. We were a newly married couple in our first home, just starting to see house prices recede away from our heavy mortgage. Less flush, too, when the tax man took an interest and claimed a dollop of it. But it took me a long time to think through all the reasons why people sometimes resented my successes.

And this, surely, is Jacob, aware of his struggles, his successes, and only too aware of the times he has been wronged. Less concerned, perhaps, with the impact he is having on Uncle Laban. And God has ways of helping us through. Sometimes he allows us to get married. I think it was Mark Twain who commended marriage for the way in which it combined maximum temptation with maximum opportunity. On the subject of listening, it also combines maximum opportunity with maximum need to learn.

I have, incidentally, just failed again. Dani had been knitting and watching a programme on house selling. She had to nip out, so she asked me to tell her whether the house was sold in the end. I heard a bit of the programme about someone having created lots of space in the property, but I am afraid I was having too much fun with this to catch the vital decision. Boo.

Anyway, as you can see, my credentials for not-listening are terrific. But marriage does help. There you are, with someone from a completely different background, with alternative views on money and, indeed, everything else, and you are given however many years it is until death do-you-part to work out what the other person is thinking. Their part of the game is to communicate this by talking to you, and you have to learn to listen. This educational opportunity latent in marriage does not seem to work the other way round, since your wife always knows exactly what you are thinking, anyway.

Sometimes we come up against the stoppers at work – or in the neighbourhood, or at church. Sometimes we never really work out what is going on and stagger from fractured relationship to fractured relationship, from job to job, from church to church.

And you meet people like that, don't you? People with a clear set of grievances, people who are sure that if only they had not had to work with so-and-so, or had only someone else been in charge of the youth work, everything would still be fine.

Repairing relationships

So how does God help Jacob with his relationships? In each

case, God brings Jacob back to face up to the situation. At this stage, it may have looked to Jacob as though he has escaped Esau by running away, but he is not going to get away from Laban so easily. Although God intervenes to ensure that Laban does Jacob no harm (Gen 31:24 and 29), Jacob will be overtaken and brought to book. And although we have seen how aggressive Jacob is in putting his own case, his initial reaction to Laban's charges is quite defensive. Perhaps the message is beginning to sink in.

The repair job here is really limited to a truce – but that is progress. Jacob's way of leaving the relationship, raw and angry, is no model for other relationships, and particularly not a model for any relationship with God. As with Jacob, I guess not every relationship will pan out smoothly in the end. Sometimes you can only close it down with an agreement to go separate ways. Even Paul couldn't agree with Barnabas (Acts 15:36-40), or persuade Apollos (1 Cor 16:12). But often, the repair can be much better, as we shall see with Esau.

In a sense, the episode with Laban is a subplot in a broader story about Jacob being reconciled to Esau, which again is a subplot in the grand reconciliation between Jacob and his God. For many of us, this is really good news. If we had to learn never to let a relationship founder we would spend our whole time walking around on eggshells. The good news, for me anyway, is that even if we upset people, it is always possible and right to go back. And, however unwillingly, that is how Jacob has to repair his relationships.

They say that when you try to run away from a relationship, you always encounter the same person in a different guise. Running away from a domineering father, perhaps, you encounter an unyielding boss, and so forth. It is not quite like that here. In a sense, Jacob's problem is not that he meets another Esau, but that he meets himself.

Jacob and Laban share a good deal of common outlook. Laban is skilfully introduced to us long before Jacob arrives. We are a whole generation earlier when Abraham's servant pulls up at Bethuel's in search of a bride for Isaac. Bethuel's son, Laban, is Rebekah's brother and he is very interested in this stranger's rich gifts (Gen 24:30): 'As soon as he had seen the nose ring, and the bracelets on his sister's arms, and had heard Rebekah tell what the man said to her, he went out to the man and found him standing by the camels near the spring.' No doubt he was also pleased to receive some of the dowry (Gen 24:53). And then Laban is happy to substitute one sibling for another on the wedding night, just as Jacob had been prepared to impersonate his brother.

For the whole of their time together, Laban and Jacob share a common aim of becoming wealthy. And each sees in the other a way to do so. To be fair to Jacob, he had tried to get away earlier, before he started in earnest on building his own flocks and herds (Gen 30:25-28). Like Jacob, Laban is never keen to let a good thing slip away and proves remarkably hard to get away from. He tried to detain Abraham's servant all those years ago (Gen 24:55) and since he attributes his recent success to Jacob, he tries to keep Jacob. Perhaps the recollection of that first attempt and failure to get away has helped Jacob to decide that he will finally make a run for it.

In some ways our world is smaller than Jacob's because he has to travel further to escape Esau. We can just move to a different church down the road. We can probably find another job without having to move house. For Jacob, he has to move a long way to make his new start. On the other hand, his world is so small that he cannot avoid Esau for the rest of his life.

Whatever we may say about how Jacob handled the parting with Laban, it was God who had told him to move on (Gen 31:13). The allusion to Bethel probably leaves Jacob in little doubt as to his final destination. Wouldn't it be nice to go straight to Bethel and worship? Again, that is not the pattern. Remember what Jesus said about worship and your brother (Matt 5:23 and 24)? 'Therefore, if you are offering your gift at the altar and there remember that your brother has something against you, leave your gift there in front of the altar. First go and be reconciled to your brother; then come and offer your gift.'

And so, off the back of his explosive parting with Laban, Jacob discovers that Esau stands between him and Bethel. Perhaps the waves of gifts carry a subscript to the more obvious message of appeasement (Gen 32:3-21). Perhaps they also say that Jacob believes the blessing has already come true for him. Perhaps they say that Esau's wealth is not at risk from the returning exile. Perhaps Jacob is trying in some way to rise above the situation in which he was enmeshed twenty years ago.

However it is, God brings Jacob back to Esau and, surprisingly, the animosity he expected seems to have evaporated. Esau is sunny and welcoming. In fact, he seems the more generous of the two. Perhaps Jacob suspects that the good times will not last if they pitch up too close together. When we were doing this as group study, Bryan felt there was more to it than that. And indeed, when the text describes Jacob's failure to follow on behind Esau to Seir as agreed, it says, 'Jacob, however, went to Succoth...' (Gen 33:12-17).

Why 'however'? Perhaps, once again, Jacob has gone as far as he can in reconciliation, but maybe he has not gone all the way. Sometimes our non-Christian relations can be more tolerant, more easy in their relationships than we. True, Esau is free of any responsibility toward God. His life is his own and he can do as he pleases. He has had the place to himself with his aging father presumably playing less and less of a role for twenty years now. But still, after all his blessings, after amassing such wealth, surely Jacob can trust God even if he ends up living near Esau.

Maybe Jacob should have been more direct with Esau and explained that he was bound for Bethel, not Seir, and perhaps they could meet up later. Perhaps he is still not free of the weakness to let potential difficulties slip by. Esau will find out in time that Jacob is not going there. Jacob will face that problem when it comes.

And so (skipping ahead), Jacob reaches Bethel (Gen 35:6). Jacob is not yet master of the repaired relationship, but he is doing so much better than before. He has had the rockiest of times with his uncle but they have parted with a truce. The relationship with Esau that threatened his life at one stage is at least at peace.

And where does this leave us? Can we understand why John thinks you must be able to handle relationships with the people you can see if you are to have a meaningful relationship with God? Relationships are the baskets in which God delivers our blessings.

Our relationships

So what can we glean from Jacob's experience on the subject of relationships? First, it is better to keep them in good repair than to have to attempt a massive repair when they are close to breaking. Notice how old some of the issues are for both Esau and Laban, when they finally explode.

The New Testament is pretty hot on maintaining our relationships. Jesus reminds us that our relationship with our brother is more important than our offering (Matt 5:23 and 24). He
also outlines a phased strategy for dealing with the person who
wrongs you. Your first approach is to the person alone, then in
front of witnesses and, finally, when all else fails, before the
church (Matt 18:15-17).

In a very practical passage (Rom 12:9-21), Paul returns again
and again to the theme of personal relationships: 'Be devoted to
one another in brotherly love. Honor one another above your-
selves... Practise hospitality...Live in harmony with one another.
Do not be proud, but be willing to associate with people of low
position... Do not repay anyone evil for evil. Be careful to do
what is right in the eyes of everybody. If it is possible, as far as
it depends on you, live at peace with everyone. Do not take
revenge, my friends, but leave room for God's wrath, for it is
written: "It is mine to avenge; I will repay," says the Lord.'

I like the passage in Romans, because as well as telling us
what to do, it gives some clues as to how to do it. For instance,
a relationship in which we are sharing with others, being hos-
pitable to others and sharing in their joys and sorrows (Rom
12:13,15), is likely to be one where love is sincere and where we
live at peace (Rom 12:9,16,18). Sharing, hospitality and spending time with people in their ups and downs are all very
achievable things.

Jacob would have done better to learn how to avoid closing
the relationships down in the first place. A boss from whom I
learned a lot helped me in this respect. Something would happen
and I would compose a magnificent reply. He would read it, tell
me it was a wonderful letter and then encourage me to put it into
the bin. Writing it was important for me, he would say (and he
had found it useful to write such missives himself from time to
time) but it would only close down the relationship. There
would be no way back from that letter. Such letters were great for
getting the angst out of your system, but their proper destination
was the bin. Now, try writing a letter that expresses your concerns, but keeps the relationship open. Better still (and he was
very hot on this), visit or phone instead of writing.

However, if Jacob's story simply told us not to mess up our
relationships, it would be of limited value, since we have all

been party to a wrecked relationship. The good news is that Jacob shows us that it is necessary and possible to repair relationships if they go wrong. So often, we feel helpless once a relationship has gone sour. God forces Jacob to return and face up to the people he has fallen out with. They do not always turn into wonderfully rewarding relationships, but they are at least workable again.

I remember a church I left with unfinished business. It got very complicated and I did some stupid things, but essentially I found myself in conflict with the leadership over the role of the young people and on the membership policy. I had left to move to a different part of the country but got thinking about it afterwards. Although I still felt I had a case (much more so then than I do, looking back, now), I realised that the relationship was not in good repair, and so I wrote to the elders. I cannot remember what I wrote but I remember meeting the elder in charge of the church a while afterwards. The letter had perplexed him to begin with. He wondered why I was trying to rake up the past. However, as he read it, he realised that I was trying to put the relationship back onto a more positive footing, and we had a very friendly chat. Incidentally, it took me a long time to put that sort of relationship based thinking into my working life.

Perhaps that it why Jesus commends the peacemakers (Matt 5:9). We do not always feel we know what to do to get things back on the rails. Sometimes someone else is able to bring us together. From my limited experience of trying to be a peacemaker, I have concluded that it is not my gifting. Certainly, if you end up as the go-between, taking messages back and forth, you are in for a long and dispiriting career. I also suspect that good peacemaking takes a bit of setting up. So how much of our time goes into identifying the peacemakers in our churches?

Finally, Jacob reminds us how easy it is to recreate essentially the same situation even though the people and initial circumstances are very different. New leaves, no matter how well turned over, are no guarantors of success. Perhaps there is some encouragement here to look back and see if any patterns have recurred over and over again in our lives. If so, the good news is that we can probably break free of the pattern by taking it back to God for repair.

Thinking it through

1. Your mother has just died and left the bulk of her estate to your younger sister who was always her favourite. How do you behave when you meet up?

2. You are planning for Christmas. You would like to visit Uncle Pat, but he always winds you up and you end up making a fool of yourself. How can you escape the clutches of repeated history this year?

3. A young person confides in you that she struggles in her Christian witness at home. She is reading her Bible and praying, but loses her temper three or four times a week. Her family finds this quite amusing, but how can you help her?

4. You had a run-in with the contracts manager last week. Your boss backed you and the contracts manager had to back down, but will not speak to you any more. What should you be doing?

5. Your boss joined you while you were talking to a customer, got the wrong end of the stick, and ended up seriously embarrassing you. He has decided to take the customer out for lunch, leaving you behind. How will you spend lunchtime?

6. Someone is applying for membership at your church. You can see that God is working in her life, but saw her walk out of the newsagents carrying three novels under a newspaper, none of which she had paid for. What should you do?

7. Think of a successful peacemaker at church. Think about the last three reconciliations he or she assisted with. What can you learn?

8. List four people you are on the outs with. If you could see the relationship restored, what would be the best that could happen as a result? What is the bare minimum level of relationship you would be happy with? Now what are you going to do in each case?

9. 1 John 5:16 tells us to pray for friends whom we see sinning. Describe a time when you have seen this work.

6

Father of the Family

Families today, certainly in the West, are more fragmented than they have been for at least a couple of generations, perhaps more than they have ever been. So many families have children with a parent outside home. School letters are sent to the parent or carer. An increasing number of grandparents, having brought up one generation, are now effectively engaged in repeating the task with the next.

Whatever the moral dimension, the fact remains that many people have chaotic personal lives. They find themselves stretched to meet the needs of more than one family; they must manage considerable financial stress; they endure difficult inter-personal relationships with old and new lovers; and they must make tricky decisions for their children with distant, sometimes hostile ex-partners, all the while trying to hold down stressful and demanding jobs. The scene for children reflects this, with an increasing number having a choice over which parent they pre-fer or which partner they like less. The instability of the family, the need to accommodate new carers and/or siblings, the large number of women left to fend for themselves and their children – all this creates a very complex fabric to our society.

And fatherhood itself is taking a bit of a battering. At the extreme end, any woman who wants a life free of men finds she can do so perfectly well – even procreating using a sperm bank. In the media, old-fashioned fathers are often resented for their overbearing chauvinism, modern-day fathers maligned for their fecklessness. The papers contain a steady trickle of darker sto-ries as abusive fathers or step-fathers reach the courts. The new father, hailed faintly from the wings as society becomes vague-ly aware of some sort of parenting gap, emerges blinking and uncertain into the spotlight, prepared to divide any parenting task into two equal parts and fulfil his 50% of the bargain. I am not saying that new fathers are any better or worse than old fathers – merely that the genre is having something of an iden-tity crisis.

A modern Jacob

And there are elements of each of these in Jacob's story. In a world that accepted polygamy, Jacob had two wives and also slept with the servant of each. Whether this broke up into four separate family groups, each with its own tent or household, or whether they tended to aggregate around Leah and Rachel is not clear to me. It looks like Hagar, two generations before, remained as Sarah's servant even after she conceived Abraham's son (Gen 16:1-16). However, by the time Joseph is in his late teens (Gen 37:2), Bilhah's and Zilpah's sons seem to be a separate group, perhaps a pair of groups. This passage also hints at tensions due to status, as the lower status sons take on a greater share of the shepherding. In the final blessing (Gen 49), all six of Leah's sons are listed first. Compounded with this are the tensions of age, where Leah's well-established family has its act together while the younger sons of the favoured wife are still growing up. And the sisters are at war with each other as they vie for Jacob's affections.

In all this, Jacob comes across as a little distant, almost indifferent, coming in from the fields to discover the sleeping arrangements have been changed (Gen 30:14-16), or failing to respond when he hears that Reuben has been to bed with Bilhah (Gen 35:22). Society may have accorded Jacob a role of respect as the head of his family, but life can carry on without him, it seems, and sometimes he appears to lack the energy to resist its flow. Furthermore his formal position of authority appears tacitly to have been undermined on many occasions, whether by Rachel stealing Laban's household gods (Gen 31:19), or with the older brothers lying to their father about Joseph's fate (Gen 37:31 and 32).

Background summary

So let us recap to remind ourselves how this state of affairs arose. Having worked seven years to pay Rachel's dowry, Jacob enters the wedding tent a happy man, only to discover by the light of day that the woman he imagined to have been Rachel was actually Leah (Gen 29:21-26) who has been given Zilpah as her maidservant. Jacob remonstrates with Laban who cites a custom about younger daughters not being married off first and offers him Rachel as a second wife, for a further seven years labour, as soon as a week's honeymoon is complete. Jacob agrees to this and is soon married to Rachel, too, who also receives a maidservant from her father, Bilhah. It helps if you can remember which servant goes with which sister – my only way is to recall that they match if you put the servants in reverse alphabetical order. Thus, Leah who comes before Rachel in the dictionary, receives Zilpah who comes alphabetically after Bilhah.

My reading of Genesis 29:31 indicates that perhaps nothing much happens to begin with, as Rachel enjoys the bulk of her new husband's attention. After that, Leah bears Jacob four sons – Reuben, Simeon, Levi, and Judah (Gen 29:31-35). Rachel becomes desperate and tries to build her side of the household through Bilhah, who bears Jacob two more sons, Dan and Naphtali. It seems that these events corresponded with a barren patch for Leah who decides that Zilpah can also bear children on her behalf – Gad and Asher (Gen 30:4-13).

Later, in an amazing piece of bargaining between the sisters, Leah negotiates to have Jacob's bed for the night (Gen 30:14-18). Jacob falls in line and Leah conceives a fifth son, Issachar. Leah continues to bear children, and eventually her brood numbers six sons and a daughter, with the addition of Zebulun and Dinah (Gen 30:19-21).

Finally, God remembers Rachel and she bears Joseph (Gen 30:22-24). Then she dies in childbirth after the whole family has left Laban and has passed on from Bethel, and Benjamin becomes Jacob's youngest son (Gen 35:16-18). Getting the exact chronological order of all the children is not easy, but is not that important, either.

It is hard to read the story without a sense of tragedy. Leah is perhaps the most tragic character, from that first night when her husband thinks she is someone else, through years of taking second place, struggling with her sister, failing to win Jacob over despite bearing son after son in a society that valued sons highly. Does Leah have any moral responsibility for her own plight? Did she ever consider letting Jacob know who she was on that fateful evening? Was she too afraid of her father to say anything? Did she see herself as having any rights in the situation? Did she want Jacob to find out? Certainly, throughout her marriage, what little we know of her shows her to have been a woman of courage, fortitude, and integrity.

Although it would have been almost impossible for Jacob to

have found it, there was a course of action that would have saved him a great deal of his share in this tragedy, namely remaining monogamous with Leah. If we had asked him, however, it is more likely that he would have seen himself married to an extra wife, not of his own choosing, and have seen very little way around it. Although Jacob must bear some responsibility for the events, given the trickery of his uncle, it is hard to see Jacob as the villain of the piece. As he is drawn into Rachel's struggles, he opens another can of worms, doubling the number of his partners. I am not sure that it takes that much imagination to guess that Jacob may have seen himself in his sexual relationships as a victim of circumstances to some extent. And to some extent, Jacob is always content to drift into a relationship, resisting it when it becomes too constraining, breaking free, often in a big show down. But these relationships do not lend themselves to the big dust-up at the end.

When I was growing up, I remember an older Christian telling me that Rachel was a real problem for Jacob. At the time, I liked the idea that beautiful Rachel had been the right one for Jacob all along and that the pair had been wickedly cheated by Laban with his substitution of the ugly Leah. But what little evidence we have points the other way. Rachel, beautiful as she is, is the one who steals her father's household gods. She must have known that Jacob could not approve such an action – as a monotheist and as someone who takes a scrupulous attitude to what belongs to himself and to his uncle.

After that, it is much harder to read. Does she rule the roost, pushing her sister as far to the periphery as she can? Given the situation, is it possible to imagine any existence other than drawn-out conflict between them? The woman desperate to have children sharing the range with her sister who bears child after child, must have found this outcome a bitter pill to swallow. The text indicates that God had a hand in all this but either Jacob is too pre-occupied with other things, or Rachel is still too attached to another view of faith to realise what is going on here. And her story ends so sadly, too, dying in childbirth and calling her boy, 'Son of my Sorrow'. Jacob cannot live with that and renames him Benjamin, 'Son of my Right Hand'.

Leah's daughter Dinah is another tragic character. Violated on her first date, she is the unwitting subject of devastating retribution and appears to remain single for the rest of her life. What do we make of the story? How on earth would you start to put the pieces back together again?

Can all the pieces ever be put back together again?

Husband and wife

Despite the fact that he has lots of women in his life, Jacob comes across as quite a lonely character, making his most difficult decisions alone. When he is near to dying, perhaps we catch the wistfulness of a relationship that got close in the end, when he requests that his sons bury him in the cave of Machpelah: 'and there I buried Leah' (Gen 49:31). Jacob's married life is so complex and fraught that it is hard to draw much from it, until we remember how many marriages are not a million miles from this in terms of complexity, mixed parentage, and competitive relationships.

In Jacob's case, less would certainly have been a great deal more.

If Jacob has anything to say to us, it is surely on the desirability of keeping things simple. Leah is perhaps a better model, here, building her family, living within the limitations of her situation and ultimately triumphing – in her case by the number of children she bears and her lifespan, which outlasts that of her younger sister. Both of these, in Old Testament times, were regarded as divine blessings. From the names of her children, she seems to be aware of this dimension.

After the pattern is set, there is no sudden deliverance. God does not take away the heartache, but time does ameliorate the pain. For Leah, her position is steadily strengthened and presumably becomes bearable. I guess it is often those long periods of graft and hard grind that, in retrospect, have brought forth the most fruit. Lots of relationships have been a little bit like that – where the tempestuous years have given way to quieter years and, where there is a commitment to keep it all together under God, to a happier retirement.

One of the best ways of discovering this it to talk to retired Christian couples. It is a great encouragement. With some free time a couple of weeks ago, I decided to visit an older couple from church. They are coming up to their diamond anniversary and are sufficiently relaxed about themselves (as I find many old people are) to be honest about life. As we chatted, I could see that they had had it very tough at times and some days had brought them sad surprises. Despite their faith, there had been no magical escapes. Endurance had been the key and now, with their first great-grandchild on the way, comfortable in their bungalow, time had brought a sense of peace and reward in the end.

I guess Jacob's experience is not the best place to find out about really rewarding marriage. There are other parts of scripture where you are likely to learn much more of the potential of a great marriage. But the message from Jacob is that the unbearable can become tolerable and in retrospect really fruitful, under the hand of God.

More broadly, marriage is full of those long-term issues. The handicapped child, the recurring bouts of illness, the debilitating disease. Endured in faith and good cheer, they may help to develop character and turn out to be great times when we look back on them. There is a story of Churchill that I have not checked, which relates to a school song. Presumably referring to the war years, the author had written of darker days. Churchill asked to change the word 'darker' to 'sterner' (Or was it 'dark' to 'stern'?), explaining that they were not dark days but great days. And so they were.

Work and ambition

Wherever he looks, Jacob's life is stressed. At work, there are constant tensions with his uncle and employer and, in time, with his cousins (Gen 31:1,38-42). On top of the tensions, it was sheer hard work – relentless, sweaty, freezing at night, sapping, sleep-depriving and generally a very hard slog.

And when he comes home, what is there? More strife! One day he comes home to discover that the household is all excited about some mandrake plants that Reuben has found. Since Reuben is Leah's son, this find, believed to have magical powers, belongs to Leah – and Rachel is desperate to try them. Jacob discovers that he is part of the bargain by which Rachel gets the plants and Leah gets to sleep with Jacob. How does Jacob feel about all this?

Again, it is a hard one to call, but putting the whole picture together and observing how his older sons, in particular, get their act together and generally do things their way, we might guess that Jacob lets the mess at home drift along and puts most of his energy and ingenuity into the flock. It is only a guess and it may be unfair to Jacob.

But it is a tension that faces men today, too. The pressure of work, of getting in early, of being one of the last to leave, of having to come up continually with new and innovative ways of improving performance. For many there is that daily grind of just getting to work, with hours a day wasted on a train, or on the motorway. I cannot imagine how working mothers bear the same strains and a greater share of cooking, housework and caring for the family.

But there it is. Does Jacob get the balance wrong? Does he go for this balance to escape the tensions at home? I think this part of Jacob's story comes with a call to every parent, and fathers in particular, to re-evaluate where they are investing their energies. I am not saying it would have been easy, but there were issues at home that nobody else could have addressed. If Jacob saw anything of his own sibling rivalry in the relationship between Leah and Rachel (inverted perhaps by his clear preference for the younger of the sisters), he appears to do little to bring some fairness into the home.

And it is hard to get fully involved in the home after a hard day's work. Particularly when the children are young, the end of the day arrives with both parents looking for some relief. Mum may have had the children all day and they have nearly driven her crazy. Dad has had a rough time and wants to put his feet up. Each sees in the other the answer to a desperate need, and both will be disappointed.

I can only speak as a father, but it is hard to switch off from the day behind and join in with the train set, or listen patiently to your child read. Sometimes it is hard to remember that your child is not making a presentation for the board's approval. He or she is just trying to learn to read. It is hard not to keep returning to that key decision that you think will make all the difference to the family. Surely it will be much easier all around if you could only swing that promotion.

Of course, with communication systems, absence is not quite the problem it was. In one year, I worked out that I had spent over a month of nights away from home. Looking back, it had an impact on the family and on my participation at church. There were some up-sides, too. I probably read more around that time than in any decade of my life. Also, Dani and I eventually got on top of the phone and we used to joke that we communicated better when I was away than when I was at home. After I learned to forget about the cost of transatlantic calls, we could have ten or fifteen minutes a day and chat through things in a way we might not have done had we both been at home.

But it may be that you decide that the goals at work are not worth the effort demanded. Maybe you find yourself having to choose. My guess is that the key choice does not lie in going after this job or that job. I think the key choices are the small ones – perhaps deciding to play Yahtzee after tea with your children, committing yourself to reading and praying with them whenever you are in, and setting a pattern. Your own stress levels will tell you how much you can fit around that.

Not that I am close to being an ideal parent. Nor am I holding up the close parenting of our culture and age, as the ideal. Nelson Mandela (*Long Walk to Freedom*) says how dumbfounded he was to hear the nature and number of questions white children asked, and to discover the unfailing willingness of white parents to answer them. Different eras, different places, different parenting models.

The tension between personal ambition (or even survival in the workplace) and providing enough time for the family is extremely difficult – in any age or under any culture. However, there are some good books on the market and time invested there will help you work through this area.

But I think you can go one better. For me, the interesting approach is to work it out for yourself – to take Jacob's example and think about it, pray about it, carry it around in your back pocket and mull it over in odd moments, on the train, in the car. Of course this will involve reading the text over, time and time again. Let it sink in until your mind is comfortable with the narrative and recalls those small, insightful, twists in the pattern. And slowly, as you do so, I believe Jacob will emerge for you as a rounded, real person whose struggles as a father will parallel your own. As you do this, ask yourself the question, 'How like Jacob am I?' How much of the remoteness from his family was preventable? How much of that is replicated in my life? How accessible am I to my family? How much does my work, my ministry even, my striving for success, get in the way of being a good father? I am not suggesting that the choices were easy in Jacob's life, but they will be hard for us, too. And we must recognise that Jacob enjoyed considerable success as a father, in the end.

For I don't want to leave you with the wrong impression. Ultimately, Jacob overcomes the early setbacks and sees his entire family established on a lifestyle that will bring them blessing, too. I do not believe that Jacob is a bad father. He is a stressed father, he is a worried father, he has to keep too many plates spinning, and his decisions sometimes suffer in consequence. The great thing about Jacob is that he has a great God and God sorts his family out in time, too.

Jacob and his sons

Although my Mom is an American, she has now spent more time in the UK than anywhere else, and got the bug for British history, reading widely. I remember her telling us a story she had been reading about Lady Astor (another American who found she liked Britain) on the campaign trail. A working-class mother complained that her children were just as good as Lady Astor's. The campaigner's response was to ask which of her children she had in mind. Lady Astor explained that some of her children had certainly behaved badly – but there might be one child who really was better than this lady's children.

And it is like this with Jacob. His great success as a father surely lies in the education he gives Joseph, providing him with enough truth and introducing him to a sufficiently personal relationship with God to sustain the teenager through the most appalling experience of betrayal and ill treatment. Although Joseph is still a teenager (Gen 37:2), with all the arrogance and assurance that came from his privileged position in his father's affections, he has a working faith. It needs time to develop and mature, but like the grain of mustard seed (e.g. Matt 13:31 and 32) it has that capability to grow. The great thing about mustard seeds is not that they are small, but that they grow. And Jacob, with a great deal less time than he imagined he had, provides Joseph with a spiritual start in life that works.

Favourites

We are all aware of the downside of the favouritism that nearly ruins Joseph as a person. You would have thought that Jacob, of

all people, would have discouraged favouritism. Perhaps he felt
he had managed to do so for the first ten sons. However it was,
Jacob reproduces the same environment under which he suf-
fered as a child. Although Isaac's success in imparting a working faith to his younger twin, Jacob, is a massive achievement,
we have also noted the way in which he favoured Esau.

I remember getting into a yellow cab in California and starting to chat to the driver. I asked how business was doing and the
driver just exploded. He gave me a tirade about how white collars like me always wanted to pretend that blue collars were
doing OK. I gathered that home life was pretty squalid. After
ripping into me for a while he calmed down and then said one
of the saddest things I have ever heard. He said that he had been
born in poverty and that he had recreated it around him.

And I guess it can be like that. We may not like the way our
parents did things, but we may just as easily fall into the same
patterns, even when we set out to do things very differently. For
instance, if our father was a hands-off parent, we may decide to
get closely involved with our children. However, even then, we
may repeat a broader pattern, perhaps by being indulgent, highly critical, or overbearing with our children.

Of course there is a positive side to this. Our children may
decide to do everything very differently from us and yet take
our approach and principles into this act of independence. In
our family, I think the brother who most struggled with my Dad
as we grew up, has turned out to be most like him in terms of
his values and commitment. And that has to be success.

And the message for us? Perhaps there is a call to take stock
of our own aspirations as parents, to review the way in which
we are bringing up our children and to free ourselves of the prej-
udices we inherited or reacted to as we started off as parents.

Crowd control

Of course, it does not work out as easily for the other brothers,
by and large. Perhaps their labour was needed early on in their
lives, especially once Jacob had to manage his own flock without prejudice or loss to Laban's property. I think one of the reasons the Marx brothers were so anarchic was that there were
several of them. In *Groucho*, Stefan Kanfer's biography of Groucho Marx, he relates a story of the three brothers, Chico, Harpo

and Groucho, having trouble getting time in their producer's diary (p 191). Thalberg was a busy man. The first time they were kept waiting, they blew cigar smoke under his door, yelling, 'Fire!' The next time, they were left in his office while he disappeared to negotiate with Louis B Mayer. Thalberg returned to find the three actors, starkers, roasting potatoes in his display fireplace. On the third occasion, his office took an hour to break into because the brothers had barricaded the door with filing cabinets. After that, they always got their audience. I am not sure that a single actor behaving that way would have succeeded in anything other than embarrassing himself and being thrown out for good measure, if not for good.

Apart from guessing at how the household ticked from the hints in the sparse narrative that covers twenty years, we see the results of Jacob's early parenting. Jacob's disability, received at Peniel, may have had a positive effect on his family. Perhaps it was their first glimpse of what a real God could do. Also, it puts an end to Jacob's days in the fields. He moves well and truly into management.

Perhaps it is reading too much into the passage to see some measure of crowd control in Jacob's approach, but in Genesis 37:2, the sons of Bilhah and Zilpah are herding one flock. The other sons also spend their days in the fields since, when Joseph is captured (Gen 37:14-28), Reuben and Judah are mentioned by name. Has Jacob started to realise that this power block needs careful management? Has he started, where possible, to split them up, so that different groups manage different herds?

Whatever his approach, Jacob tends to let things run, avoiding conflict. And there is plenty to get upset about. Reuben goes to bed with Bilhah (Rachel's maidservant and the mother of two of his half-brothers). Jacob hears but apparently does nothing (Gen 35:22). Jacob is so used to playing the long game that he does not act quickly, even when it is within his own family. Maybe he is afraid the showdown will go against him since Reuben's motives must surely have contained an element of defiance (compare it with Absalom's approach in 2 Sam 16:22). Who knows? While the long game may work outside the family, surely it would have been better to deal swiftly with this problem.

Again, when news of Dinah's rape reaches the homestead, Jacob leaves his response until his sons come home from the field. Simeon and Levi respond in a manner that has all of Jacob's hallmarks on it – deceit, and ruthlessness once a winning position was established – with a good deal of violence and bloodshed thrown in (Gen 34:1-31). Jacob is horrified at the extent of the bloodshed and afraid that the locals will gang up in revenge.

How do we evaluate this? Jacob's rebuke (Gen 34:30) seems mild when we consider the extent of the bloodshed. Presumably, the booty is accepted and Jacob, again, lets things ride for the present.

It is hard to know what Jacob really believes when his sons return to tell him that the hated Joseph has met with some unfortunate accident (Gen 37:31 and 32). When it comes time to send Benjamin to Egypt, Jacob ignores Reuben's offer to look after him and entrusts his youngest son to Judah's care (Gen 42:37-43:14 and 44:13-34) – number four in the family.

Again, time favours Jacob in the long run. He does not err in his final blessing. Reuben is passed over for defiling his father's bed. Levi and Simeon are passed over, too, for their fury and cruelty. And in the end, he even gets it right with Joseph. Where better to place the blessing that would see the family through to surer times, than to give it to Joseph who had vindicated his father's early expectations by overcoming extreme obstacles and had risen to international prominence? But Jacob does not err this time. He manages better than Isaac in getting beyond personal preference. Having passed over the first three of his sons, he gives the best blessing to number four, Judah – where it has remained (Gen 49:8-12).

Perhaps Jacob's greatest achievement as a father is that he succeeds in leading all of his family in worship at Bethel (Gen 35:1-15). Despite an unpromising start, eventually Jacob steps out in faith, tells his family to get their act together on purity, and leads them in worship.

Family worship

Given all the negative aspects of his family experience, we may undervalue Jacob's achievement as a father in leading the family to Bethel. In God's economy, however, I suspect that acts of worship such as this count for much more than we realise. Much is ignored, discounted, or forgiven the struggling father who manages to teach his family to worship in the end.

Some people make a point of having a time together each day. Maybe a reading and a prayer at breakfast. When we were young, another family had a pack of pictures of friends that they worked through at three per day and prayed as a family for their friends. My parents adopted the idea, which works well, provided you make a point of keeping up-to-date with both the pictures and the news. Others make a point of reading and praying with each child at night. We have gone for that approach, pairing up the elder two, and find it works well. The educationalists will tell you that boys often lack a good role model for reading, since few of them, apparently, see their own fathers reading. This approach, especially if Dad can find the time, works well on both counts.

You never know what questions will come up when you read a passage. The other night, it was the parable of the sower, care of Luke (Luke 8:4-15). Hang on a minute, someone wants an explanation: how can people look but not see (Luke 8:10)? His older brother had some ideas, then he had some ideas. Dad got a chance to suggest an idea or two, and then you move on. Tonight I want to go back to that, because the same somebody was discussing whether it was still a good idea to wear shorts to school. Basically, he had decided, it wasn't as cold as it looked. Most of his friends were into long trousers by now because it looked cold. But when you actually went out at playtime, it wasn't. He went on to say that he could never understand why people said that seeing is believing. 'Have you heard that saying, Daddy?' Clearly, for him, feeling was believing, and if it felt cold it was cold. If it just looked cold, it wasn't necessarily cold. So when it comes to the temperature, someone had decided you could look but not see. Stimulated by this insight, he moved on to holograms (where you can see things that are not really there) and other things. But what a view of seeing and not seeing! (Incidentally, he has a choice over his trousers – and his parents do not leave him in shorts over the winter!)

The approach suffers from the fact that you rarely pray as a family (although you can arrange it from time to time, if you try). With two older boys and one son quite a bit younger, I tend to read (first something secular, then something from the Bible) and pray with the older two and do something similar with the youngest. He wants to get in with the big boys, now, and we are exploring ways of rescheduling the evening to make this possible. It has the advantage that the youngest messes about less at prayer time when he is sharing it with the others.

And children can pray the most wonderful, creative prayers. In finding the right way forward, there are probably as many alternatives as there are Christian parents. Some set out to have a fun time, with bedtime singing, others will want to be more structured. Some will go for a weekly, rather than a daily event, and follow-up daily with their children in other ways. But it is a wonderful privilege as a parent to come with them before Almighty God and worship with them. And I suspect that many children are missing out because their parents have not yet followed Jacob in this important area.

I wonder how Jacob felt as he began, quite late in the day, to teach his family to worship. Was he a little ashamed to be starting so late? Was he at all worried that his sons might think it a little hypocritical to make a big show of worship after the previous twenty years? Or did they see that, after what God had done to tame the irate Laban, this was important – whenever you got around to it?

Perhaps, fresh from the incident of Dinah and the men of Shechem (whose wives and children presumably formed part of the great caravan over which Jacob presided), their own consciences were a little tender. Perhaps years of established behaviour were coming back to them.

It is always difficult to establish new patterns in our lives and, if a pattern appears to be one that will make us look more holy, perhaps we feel even more awkward. It may make sense to start things simply, to do something we can manage for a few minutes a day, rather than to try for something grand that will be very hard to keep up. Maybe just getting the family together at mealtimes once a day and saying grace will be the starting point that you can live with.

My guess is, that after the initial embarrassment, your offspring will probably respect the attempt to change more than they will resent it. Of course, it all depends on whether the rest of the lifestyle goes with the newfound desire to worship.

Father nonetheless

I hope you are building up a picture of a man who wrestles with a very modern set of problems. Despite his failures in some areas, he succeeds where it most matters – in bringing the family to a place of worship. At his worst, he seems a little aloof from the family, and sets a disingenuous example in his business dealings, but he has a spectacular success in assisting Joseph towards a personal walk with God.

Although time only enhances Jacob as a father, it does not untangle all the knots. The fighting between his sister-wives probably only comes to an end with Rachel's premature death, but there is some sense of peace about his last reference to Leah.

I think his successes are worth thinking through further, because we probably undervalue them. His failures? Well, they are highly instructive, especially so, since, if we are honest, they are very like our own.

Thinking it through

1. How would you know if you were getting the balance between work and home life wrong?
2. Where does the new man in society conform well to a biblical picture of fatherhood, and where does he falter? How about old-fashioned fathers?
3. A lady at Toddler Group reveals that she is living in a hostel, having been beaten up by her husband. How would you try to help, one to one? What other steps might you take?
4. How much time do you think a modern Christian father should try to spend with his children? Will it change as they grow older?
5. What are the top five things you want for your children? Looking back over Jacob's life, how many of the things you want for your children are really worthwhile?
6. When during the week do you feel least adequate as a parent? What hints or encouragement does Jacob's story offer?
7. Friends with a teenage son and daughter and a ten-year-old, ask you how they can start some family worship in steps that will actually work. How would you advise them?

8. How many hours in the past year have you spent conversing meaningfully with Christian older people? What have you gained from the experience? How will Jacob's story affect your schedule as far as meeting older people is concerned?

9. Your son has just been arrested for stealing CDs from cars one night in the town centre. What is your response?

10. Which aspects of your parents' style have you tried to copy and which have you deliberately tried to avoid? How successful do you think you have been?

11. What do your children make of your parenting?

12. In view of the Chronicler's assertion that Joseph got the rights of the firstborn (1 Chron 5:1 and 2), how do you read Jacob's blessings to Judah and Jacob (Gen 49:8-12, 22-26). Is there a degree of ambiguity left in the old boy yet?

7

By Faith, Jacob

Earlier this year, I was asked to give a sort of epilogue at the party of one of the grand old men of our fellowship who had just reached 80 although, sadly, he had not long lost his wife. I spent quite a lot of time thinking about Moses. My friend was unusual in that each of his daughters (and he only had daughters) had made a personal commitment of faith in Jesus, and each of his grandsons (and he only had grandsons) had followed suit. Somehow Moses did not seem quite to fit the bill and when the evening came round, I realised why. My friend had been thinking about Moses for his own remarks at his party that night. And then I thought about Jacob.

The last glimpse we catch of Jacob is sketched out by whoever wrote Hebrews (Heb 11:21). He writes, 'By faith Jacob, when he was dying, blessed each of Joseph's sons, and worshipped as he leaned on the top of his staff.'

The pictures come from the end of Genesis. The old man leans on his staff and worships as Joseph promises to bury him back home in the land promised to them (Gen 47:31). A little later when Joseph hears that his father has taken a turn for the worse, Jacob blesses his grandsons (Gen 48:1-20). The writer flips the historical order to leave us with a poignant picture – a very old man, supported by a stick, worshipping.

And in the end, Jacob learns to worship. He learns that his life revolves, not around wells, or even the sheep, but around Bethel. While we pay a great deal of attention today to styles of worship, Jacob reminds us of the need for our worship to have real substance. What matters is not so much how he worships, as that he worships. For Jacob, worship provides the lynchpin of his existence. Everything hangs from it. God is the star around which his life orbits, burning away lesser ambitions, illuminating a path ahead. And now Jacob sees things differently, as we shall see.

It is in his worship that Jacob differs fundamentally from Esau. Esau never learns to worship. His yearnings are all for this world, for which his talents and aspirations have prepared him so well. To begin with, it did not look as if Jacob's spiritual yearning would make that much of a difference. It did not seem to compensate for his leaner frame and meaner personality. Jacob's faith has taken a long time to mature and bear fruit but now, at last, we have a picture of Jacob as he was meant to be.

Physically drained and weakened, clinging to his crutch as he has done for years now, well aware of his infirmity, Jacob worships. The flocks he once herded have died and new generations have sprung up many times since they dominated his thinking. The children he struggled to find time for have grandchildren of their own. They are still together. The tribe, too, is learning to worship, although it will take a blinding experience of fear, rescue and isolation in a desert before it, too, learns to focus on God alone.

And although he is almost done, physically, he sees things very clearly, especially when he blesses his grandsons. Here we have a rerun of an old, old story. Two sons, one big blessing. Jacob is almost blind and when Joseph arrives with Manasseh and Ephraim, he has to ask who they are (Gen 48:8). Somehow, Jacob realises that the younger son will produce the larger tribe. Despite Joseph's best efforts to manoeuvre Jacob's right hand onto Manasseh's head and his protests as Jacob crosses his hands over to make the switch, Jacob insists on giving the younger son the better blessing.

Isaac before him had struggled to get it right, torn between this sense and that, in an attempt to understand what was happening. Jacob, similarly handicapped, is able to get things the right way round.

Nor is Jacob intimidated by Joseph, his powerful son. Years ago he might have let it ride – sort things out with a mumbled blessing perhaps, perhaps a bit of ambiguity in the wording of the blessing for each, but avoid, at all costs, a struggle you might lose. Not any more. Jacob is unfazed by it all, even though Joseph is 'displeased'. I would guess a lot of people got very worried when Joseph was displeased, but not Jacob. In the end, centuries later when the kingdom has been divided to two, the regions come to be known by their dominant tribes, Judah in the south and Ephraim to the north. Jacob got it right.

So what does this story tell us about walking with God?

A thousand years a day

First, it reminds us that God's time scales are not ours. We want things fixed this week, or in three months at most. Sometimes God is thinking decades, maybe even centuries ahead. Can we cope with that? I remember my daily reading at a time when I was really struggling at work. In fact, my early years at work were quite difficult for me, as well as being times of progress and reward. I remember looking for encouragement and, if I am honest, for a way out. My reading that day was Jesus' parable on the fig tree (Luke 13:6-9), where the owner wants to tear it down and make a fresh start. I liked that bit. Then, horrors! The gardener wants to give it a go for another year to see if it will bear fruit. Another year! I was not sure I could take another year. In the end, of course, I could and did. And some of the lessons I learned in those difficult times have opened up the way for much more rewarding times at work.

On another occasion, I remember writing to some missionary friends of mine. They were struggling and, a few years later, they returned to the UK. The amount of time they had put into Bible college and language study made it very difficult for them to contemplate coming back to England without feeling complete and utter failures. I tried to encourage them to see that good things had happened in their own spiritual development, whatever the final outcome. I also wanted them to think about the enormous privilege they had been able to offer their children of growing up bilingually, and studying in a different school system. I am not sure how much of an impact it made at the time, but now, with their bilingual children scooting ahead at school, anyone can see that they have given the next generation an education that they could never have afforded to buy them. I was encouraged in this line of thinking when talking it over with a godly old boy at church who simply wondered whether all this might have been for their children.

If you are amazingly ancient, I hope this encourages you to pray for your grandchildren. I think it is an old Jewish joke that asks why children get on so well with their grandparents. The answer is that they have a common enemy. I know that opportunities are not there as they once were for many, but telephones and even e-mail open up new ways to communicate. So many younger people today are looking for support and a listening ear. Jacob provides a powerful perspective on the passage of years. The themes take years to mature. They do in our world. I have no idea what the world will be like when the majority of the population reaches maturity with little or no experience of a stable home. I am sure that God sees it coming and, even now, is sowing the seeds of salvation in the face of disaster.

Jacob reminds us to hold tight and assures us that, even when things look desperate, God can bring peace in the long run. Holding tight to God will bring the peace even more quickly.

Not everything works out well. It is hard to see that Bilhah, Zilpah or even Dinah, had a ball. But we know so little about their lot that we cannot say more. We know that God took time out to reassure Abraham's concubine, Hagar, that he was looking after her needs when she reached low ebb (Gen 16:7-14). In fact, Hagar was so surprised that God should even be aware of her that she says, 'You are the God who sees me.' We simply do not know God's arrangements for these others, but can be confident that God was watching over them, too.

But even still, there are loose ends. Is the tribe finally ready to worship? Well, in places, but it takes another great man, trained and toned, again over many decades, to lead them out to meet their God. In the meantime, Joseph has learned to worship and Jacob has the privilege of blessing the next generation down.

Just understanding that God's plans stretch out and out for years, decades, into time unforeseeable, has always been a great comfort to God's people. I love Psalm 102, where the poet struggles with his own problems for a while and then remembers that God looks after the heavens and has a purpose for them, to bring even them to an end, as you might fold away a well worn shirt.

My academic interview is the day after tomorrow. Will it really matter in the great swirl of things? Does this decision, critical as it seems to the family and me, does it really matter? Well, yes and no. Yes, because God really does care. As Hagar discovered, he really does watch over our family. But no, because I cannot really get this one wrong. He has plenty of time to apply a correction factor if I mess up. Maybe one of the boys will fill the gap I create by accident. Who knows? The big time frame stops us from stewing over details.

Model parents

And that is the second thing that Jacob reminds us of. It is very hard to go wrong when we truly worship. Did you read the verse before Jacob's verse in Hebrews (Heb 11:20)? It says, 'By faith Isaac blessed Jacob and Esau in regard to their future.'

Amazed? I am. Isaac appears to have given in to a rose-tinted view of his elder son. But he worships and, although the course of events is horribly convoluted, he, too, gets it right in the end. He ends up blessing the right son in the right way. So often, our foibles are completely invisible to us. We cannot see that our habit of exaggerating actually makes forays into the territory of deception at times. We may not see that our love of cars is squandering money that could be better spent elsewhere. We may not see that our concern over those creeping wrinkles will only focus our attention on a game we can only lose, and away from the only game we are bound to win. And God is so often gracious and responds to the faith he finds in the rest of our lives. I am not sure any of us grasp what a truly wonderful thing faith is to God, how much dross he will dispose of for a grain of faith. And despite his failing, Isaac got the really important decision right.

And so does Jacob. Despite his struggles as a father (and we focus too much on failure), here he is with his grandsons. Jacob reminds us that it is never too late to start pulling the family together and heading off to worship. Whatever has happened in the past, Jacob enjoys a position of prestige inside, and even outside, the family. And it is not just that Jacob hung in there. Had God not been at work, Reuben, Simeon and Levi might well have taken the clan off raiding and pillaging.

Perhaps you feel you have blown it as a father. Your witness to the family when it was young was variable and now that you have a clutch of teenagers, they want nothing of your world. I cannot provide the advice here, since my family is younger than that. Families that I have seen hold together through the teenage years have tended to be open, honest and relaxed. It is amazing how many rebellious teenagers come round in the end. Provided there are still parents to pray for them, and give them support when they reach the point of turning, it may be OK for them, too, in the end.

Maybe your phase in life involves starting all over again with the grandchildren, taking them to church with you and worshipping with the next generation down.

I remember it being said about one chess champion that you

had to beat him three times in every game. You had to beat him in the opening, you had to beat him in the middle game and you had to beat him at the endgame. And Jacob seems to say that parenting is a bit like that. Just because you mess up the opening, or even the middle game, it does not stop you from winning the endgame. Dig in there, renew your worship, and see what God can do for you as a parent.

Person to person

Third, Jacob reminds us that relationships are important. Ultimately all God has for us is a relationship. The most profound description of God, 'God is love' (1 John 4:8,16), is couched entirely in the language of relationship. The world around us has some concept of the importance of relationships. We have no end of seminars on customer relationship management, relationship building, relationship selling, and so forth. Most of the time it fails because they get the people-bits wrong. Your bank sends you an invitation for a new credit card just after you have had the most amazing struggle to get it to re-issue the one you lost on holiday in Vietnam. Or maybe your utility company tells you how important you are when you ring in and strings you along for fifteen minutes, pressing buttons like an idiot and listening to snatches of Vivaldi. Perhaps your library tells you that, to improve your experience of borrowing books, they will be closed on Tuesday mornings for staff training. I actually received a customer care call recently from a chap who could not listen to my views at all until I had answered yes or no to a string of irrelevant questions.

God is after relationships – with the people included. Dani thinks it is funny that I am writing about listening and relationships, tap tapping away on the dining room table, ignoring the hubbub around me. The kids are just glad that I am not singing as well. My point in writing this is that relationships are important. I am not claiming to be brilliant at relationships. I have some relationships that go back years. I have forged some relationships in the past few years that I hope will be going strong in decades to come. But the key thing I want to encourage you to do is to look to your own relationships.

People who are good at a thing are not always good at writing about it. I may be alone in this, but I did not find that George

Müller's biography gave me any deep insights into prayer. I believe that is because his faith and prayer life were, to some extent, a gift. The thing to do with a gift, according to Romans (Rom 12:3-8) is to exercise it, not to try to explain it to others. And I think my gift in this area will be to identify that relationships are important and to encourage you to look at the state of repair in which you are keeping yours.

Because ultimately, God wants to use your ability to relate, as the channel through which to pour more blessings than you can handle.

Safe and secure

Finally, Jacob reminds us that it is possible to be secure in life. The scene of an old man, struggling perhaps for breath, as he hauls himself up from his couch and leans on his staff to bless his grandsons, is a picture of supreme security. At that end of life, of course, it becomes clear that life itself is inherently insecure, because we die. When Dani trained as a nurse, she had to learn what characterises living things. I was surprised to discover that one of the key characteristics is that they die.

He has lived a precarious life. He has found a better way to live with the uncertainties and Jacob, in the end, is magnificent, insightful, secure.

It is very easy to feel secure and to attribute it to our faith when we are actually resting on something else. On the night before I left work at the start of the summer, it struck me how risky it all was. Prospective employers had shown interest but nothing had appeared in writing. When the first job offer came through the post with an invitation to pop in and discuss it, I suddenly felt a lot better. Had my faith picked up? No, I had picked up the mail. When I turned down the industrial job before the academic job came through, it was a really scary experience. When the HR Director in the industrial job told me he could see the attraction in the academic post and to get back to him if it did not work out, I felt great again. I could see the safety net below me once more as I let go of one trapeze and waited for the next one to rise within reach.

I believe I have exercised faith over this summer, but probably not at the times or in the ways I would have wished to. And I am still sitting on a lump of money that will stop us from starving this side of Christmas, maybe this side of Easter.

In the end, faith is not about our feelings. It is not about vicious self-examination to pare away any trace of a doubtful motive, though godly introspection is right in Christian life, and should have a regular place in our worship (1 Cor 11:28). Faith is about setting our spaceship in orbit around God's sun, letting him take us where he will. And worship is enjoying the scenery that we see from there.

Just learn to worship, and do what you like.

Thinking it through

1. How has your attitude to your home changed in the past twenty to thirty years? What is the view on property amongst the over-80s in your fellowship?
2. How many times do your children see their grandparents? What arrangements are you making for them to spend time with them in the coming year?
3. A teenager tells you that they believe you just learn to worship and then you can do as you please. How do you explore this with him or her?
4. Your daughter wants a quiet Sunday morning and is happy for you to look after the children, even if it means taking them to church. How might you rearrange your Sundays?
5. Read Psalm 78. How many of the truths Jacob discovered have been woven into the psalmist's worship here?
6. What are the top five New Testament passages on security? How are you planning for them to change your life?
7. What has most challenged or encouraged you in this book? What are you going to do about it?

8

Trusting and Doing

It has been an interesting year, and Jacob has been with me on and off for most of it. Preparing for the team exercise on Sunday mornings, working with the team as we tried to get a fix on Jacob, and then listening to the talks in May and into June. He has been there again as I have been thinking about the material over the summer and having a crack at writing it up.

Letting go of one job, seeing some options emerge, and finally, trying to decide between two of them: the academic post that will mean moving and the industrial position that will not. Talking it through with friends – Christians and non-Christians, local friends and those who are miles away. Receiving calls and e-mails from friends who are praying for our decision, or wishing us the best. Trying to think ahead and see how the move would work out.

Dani and I managed to get away on our own for a few nights and there was also a family wedding. That was exciting, with people arriving from distant places. But in the end, there was still a decision to be made.

Did Jacob, especially the younger Jacob, tend to do too much and trust too little? Could we do better? I'm not sure we could. Jacob has not helped me to draw a line between the times when I should do and when I should trust. I still get too deeply involved in all the issues and it just becomes a confusing circle. But he has taught me that, provided I can trust, provided I can honestly keep taking it back to God, it is hard to do anything detrimental.

I cannot justify the decision we came to in any logical terms, but we decided to pursue the academic post and asked God to close the doors if it was not the right one. There are certainly more doors that will have to open for this one to work out.

And then we have put time into looking at the new area. Dani has been avidly surfing the net for schools; we have spent the odd day visiting the area; we have looked at a few properties; we have put our own on the market, located some churches and

visited one last week. We have had the time, so why not? Not
that all the time has been spent around the decision. There has
been time to try to fly the kite with the boys and lots of tap, tap
tapping to write this.

A great deal of uncertainty was injected into the situation by
the tragic events of 11 September, when the World Trade Centre
was so horrifically attacked. I sat and watched the news that
afternoon and felt cold at the end of it. It will sound terrible, but
as well as thinking of the despair for the people involved, particularly for those in the airliners, I found myself wondering
whether this was a good time to be out of work.

A couple of weeks down the line and the property market
seems to have died.

So here we are, a big interview tomorrow. In one sense, it is
scary. In another sense, I am sure that God will lead us forward
into something new, or back into paths we understand. Either
way it will be fun.

And now it is a couple of days after the interview. Actually, it is
not quite a quarter to seven on a Saturday morning. Yesterday I
took the remaining paperwork over to the university and col-
lected the signed offer of employment. I am an academic!

Looking back, I had realised that an academic world would
probably suit me best. The approaches I tried before (and I did
try a couple) did not lead anywhere and soon fizzled out. And
now, after this rather uncertain path, waiting at the crossroads,
sitting in a vacuum most of the time and easing away from the
only competing offer, here it is. I guess I should have known it
would be like that – but you do not see it that way when you are
going through it.

So Jacob had his promise of blessing – what has been the
promise for me? I guess the Bible is loaded with promises. The
one that has come to mean a lot to me over the years is found in
Isaiah. In chapter 46, the prophet contrasts two different types of
religion. There is the DIY religion where you carry your own
gods about. In the case of the Israelites, they were loaded on the
back of a donkey, or bobbed about in an ox cart, presumably as
the nation trekked off into captivity. A bit like Rachel and the
household gods.

God explains that he isn't that kind of a God. He won't be a burden to his people. They will not have to carry him. No! God will carry his people, especially those who need carrying. And the promise for me? It is there in verse 4 of Isaiah 46:

> Even to your old age and grey hairs
> I am he, I am he who will sustain you.
> I have made you and I will carry you;
> I will sustain you and I will rescue you.

Thank you, Father.

Further Reading

1. Roy Clements, *The Strength of Weakness*, Christian Focus Publications, 1994

2. Mark Greene, *Thank God it's Monday*, Scripture Union, 2nd edition, 1997

3. Rob Parsons, *The Sixty Minute Father*, Hodder & Stoughton, 1995

Partnership Guides

Practical help for local church groups and individuals.
Note: all titles 216 x 135mm

A Guide to God's Family
Being Part of Your Local Church
Stephen McQuoid

A practical introduction to life in a local church. Topics covered include God's view of his family, what the family gets up to, finding your niche, joys and responsibilities, family structures, and "the awkward squad". Brief chapters are supplemented by discussion questions, and suggestions for further reading.

0-900128-22-4 / 96pp

Sharing the Good News in C21
Evangelism in a Local Church Context
Stephen McQuoid

This book looks at the changes that are taking place in our society and asks the question, how do we reach that society with the Gospel? It starts with an analysis of the lessening impact of the church at the beginning of the twenty-first century, and then suggests how individual Christians can reverse this trend by involving themselves in the lives of unchurched people so as to win them to Christ.

0-900128-25-9 / 128pp

Stephen McQuoid is the Principal of Tilsley College, which is part of the ministry of Gospel Literature Outreach. He travels widely preaching in churches throughout Great Britain as well as lecturing in the College and writing. He and his wife Debbie are involved in a church planting work in Viewpark, Uddingston, Scotland.

Jake
Just Learn to Worship!
Terry Young

This book was written by an unemployed Church Elder as he waited to find out what would happen next. In the circumstances, Jacob was a great character to study and write about. Jacob lived a tough life, full of uncertainty, whether as a third-generation nomad, a farm hand for his uncle, or waiting for an uncomfortable reunion with his elder twin. Add to this a series of turbulent relationships plus a chaotic family life, and we have a picture that is very recognisable today.

0-900128-27-5 / 108pp

Forthcoming:

After the Fishermen
How Did Jesus Train his Disciples?
Terry Young

This book considers the approaches Jesus used to train his followers and then looks around to see how relevant they are today. From a non-specialist background more as trainee than trainer, the author finds that many of Jesus' methods are still around. However, while churches may be using them, it is probably secular management training organisations that are putting them to greater use.

For anyone who has been sent on an interviewing course, or has been taught how to run a meeting or conduct an appraisal, this book is a chance to explore ways of applying that training to Christian service. Most chapters conclude with a set of questions to explore the ideas further and to help in adapting the suggestions to one's own situation.

0-900128-28-3 / 100pp approx

Terry Young was born to missionary parents who eventually returned to the Midlands where he attended the local schools and university. In 1985 he moved to Essex for a job in industrial research. More recently he has become a Professor of Healthcare systems. In 1988 he married Danielle and they have served actively in their local church. They have three boys.